AAUW Educational Foundation

¡Sí, Se Puede! Yes, We Can

Latinas in School

by Angela Ginorio
and Michelle Huston

Published by the American Association of University Women Educational Foundation
1111 Sixteenth St. N.W.
Washington, DC 20036
202/728-7602
Fax: 202/463-7169
TDD: 202/785-7777
foundation@aauw.org
www.aauw.org

Copyright 2001
American Association of University Women Educational Foundation
All rights reserved
Printed in the United States

First printing: January 2001
Art direction: Sabrina Meyers
Layout: Laurel Prucha Moran and Julie Hamilton
Editors: Susan Morse and Susan K. Dyer
Cover photo: Judy G. Rolfe

Library of Congress Card Number: 00-105233

ISBN 1-879922-24-X

In Part 2, the text by Lucha Corpi is excerpted from "Epiphany: The Third Gift," copyright 1992 by Lucha Corpi, originally published in *Latina: Women's Voices from the Borderlands,* edited by L. Castillo-Speed (New York: Simon & Schuster, 1995), and reprinted here with permission of the publisher.

033-01 01-01/7500

TABLE OF CONTENTS

Acknowledgments v

Introduction vii

Part 1: Overview of Trends of Latinas' Educational Participation 1
    Graduation Rates 1
    Suspensions 3
    Tracking and Course-Taking 3
    Standardized Test Scores 9
    Grades 9
    College Enrollment by Type of College 10
    Completion of Degrees 10
    Majors 11
    Latina/o Faculty 12
    Economic Effects of Education 12

Part 2: Characteristics of Communities Affecting Participation/Success 15
    Family 15
    Peers and Peer Groups 27
    Schools 29

Part 3: Individual Characteristics Associated with Educational Outcomes 37
    Culture and the Individual 37
    Self-Efficacy 39

Part 4: Conclusion and Recommendations 41
    Effects of Family, School, and Community on
        Educational Possible Selves 42
    Recommendations 45

Appendix A: Methodology 47

Appendix B: Summary of Data on Latinas for Selected States 49

Appendix C: Some Latina-Serving Programs in the United States .57

About the Researchers 63

Endnotes 65

Bibliography 67

AAUW Equity Library 81

Order Form 83

Foundation Board of Directors 1999-2001 84

ACKNOWLEDGMENTS

We are proud to add our names to the long list of authors who have collaborated with the American Association of University Women (AAUW) Educational Foundation in their research on gender and education. Nos honra haber sido seleccionadas para preparar el informe sobre la educación de las latinas en los Estados Unidos. (We were honored to have been selected to write the report on the education of Latinas in the United States.) Such a large responsibility could not have been carried out without the support of many people.

First we want to thank the AAUW Educational Foundation and its director of research, Pamela Haag, for choosing to focus on this important topic and for their support in all aspects of the writing, editing, and publication of this report. Thanks to the Foundation's research and publications staff, including Amy Robb, Amy Beckrich, Susan Morse, Sue Dyer, Sabrina Meyers, Julie Hamilton, and others.

For facilitating and enhancing our work in big (support and interest) and small (reference checks, book searchers, and so forth) ways we thank the staff of the Northwest Center for Research on Women: Thao Diep, Bronwen Serna, and Michelle Rodman.

For providing "not to be missed" resources, leads, and names (e-mail, phone calls, and sidewalk requests were equally honored) we thank James Soto Antony, Suzanne Brainard, Ana Mari Cauce, Melanie Domenech, Juan Guerra, Patricia McGowan, and Paula Nurius at the University of Washington, Beatriz Chu Clewell of the Urban Institute, Jennifer Garrick of the National Action Council for Minorities in Engineering, and Carlos Rodríguez at Pelavin & Associates.

For insightful comments that helped the development of various points of this manuscript we thank Gene Cota-Robles, Patricia Gándara, Guadalupe García, Elena Pereyra, Carlos Rodríguez, Maricela Sánchez, and Carlos Tovares. We also thank all the participants in the Rural Girls in Science Program from whom we have learned so much, especially Angie Moreno.

For graciously agreeing to review this manuscript at various stages we thank Guadalupe Frías, Kathie Friedman, Susan Glenn, Joycelyn Moody, Helen Remick, Angela Valenzuela, Reesa M. Vaughter, and Shirley Yee.

For enormous patience for our late night, weekend, and any time consultations and work as well as personal support we want to thank our families. Angela thanks her partner Chip Muller and daughter Emi Muller-Ginorio. Michelle thanks her partner Jim Hicks, and for friendship above and beyond the call, Jim Geldmacher.

—Angela Ginorio and Michelle Huston

INTRODUCTION

Many Hispanic people think they can't be good in science. I thought I couldn't, but I can.

—Angie Moreno, "Rural Girls in Science" participant
(Migrant Education News: 1998, p. 9)

What else has this young woman thought Latinas can't be good at? What do young people everywhere learn about the possibilities their futures hold? Where do they learn that they will be best served by becoming accountants, or computer programmers, or doctors, or secretaries, or field hands, or mothers? For whom is the list of possible selves most constrained? For whom is it nearly endless? How are these possible selves constrained, and what effects do these understandings of the world have on young people's choices as they make their way toward adulthood?

This paper explores the experiences of Latinas in the United States' educational system. We utilize the concept of "possible selves" to investigate the lives of Latinas in school, at home, and with their peers. Communities formed by families, peers, and schools provide a social context in which possible selves are imagined and changed over time. In some cases, possible selves are constrained by these contexts; in others, they are broadened. Furthermore, we suggest that elements in each of these social contexts can be education-encouraging and affirming, or education-discouraging and dismissive. This will be the focus of much of our discussion.

This first section will provide an overview of our governing concepts—Latinas, education, and "possible selves"—and trends in Latina/o educational participation. The second section is a more in-depth discussion of communities (families, peers, and primary, secondary, and postsecondary schools) and their relationship to the educational process. The third section focuses on individual traits, such as self-confidence, and explores how individual experiences are shaped by educational variables. The fourth and last section offers conclusions and recommendations for school personnel, families, and policy makers.

WHY A FOCUS ON LATINAS?

The United States is growing increasingly diverse, with the Hispanic[1] population showing—and projected to show—the most dramatic population increases in the 21st century. The Hispanic population grew more than seven times as fast as the rest of the nation between 1980 and 1990 (53 percent growth) and is projected to double from the year 2010 to 2050, from 39.3 million to 80.7 million (U.S. Census Bureau: 1993b).

The Hispanic population is also much younger than other racial and ethnic groups. Fully one-third of Hispanic Americans are under the age of 15. By the year 2030, Hispanic students will comprise an estimated 25 percent of the total school population, at 16 million. This trend, while especially pronounced in California and Texas, is occurring in all major cities and urban public schools throughout the nation (President's Advisory Commission: 1996). The Hispanic American population between the ages of 5 and 13 years is projected to increase by 47 percent between 2000 and 2020, whereas the African American population of children aged 5 to 13 years is projected to increase by 15 percent. The White population of 5- to 13-year-olds is projected to decrease by 11 percent in the same period (U.S.

Department of Education: 1997). Latinas now constitute the largest "minority" group of girls in the United States, not including those living in the Commonwealth of Puerto Rico.

Substantial demographic shifts are increasing the presence of Hispanics in the United States population—especially in public schools. Yet graduation rates, college enrollment, and traditional achievement figures—among other, less quantifiable indicators—suggest that public schools are currently not meeting the needs of this growing, and diverse, student population. Notwithstanding increases in educational achievement, Latina/os continue to lag behind other ethnic minorities and Anglos on most measures of success, including educational attainment and its extension, economic well-being (Adelman: 1999; Secada, Chávez-Chávez, García, Muñoz, Oakes, Santiago-Santiago, & Slavin: 1998). Latinas, for example, comprise fully 25 percent of the female population of California, yet 61 percent of Latinas aged 25 to 44 have no high school diploma, 24 percent are graduates, and 15 percent have gone on to postsecondary education (Latino Coalition for a Healthy California: 2000). In 1999 the U.S. Secretary of Education Richard Riley proclaimed the educational achievement of Hispanic Americans a national priority (Riley Cites: 1999).

Research and data on Hispanic Americans, however, rarely focus on how students within this generic group differ by country of origin, class, region, or, more relevant for this paper, gender. Because national data are rarely disaggregated by sex and race and ethnicity, we know little about how the educational needs, achievements, or problems for Hispanic males may differ from those of Hispanic females.

This paper will review the educational status of Latinas, both in comparison with their male counterparts and in comparison with their peers in other racial and ethnic groups.

WHAT DO WE MEAN BY "LATINAS"?

When researchers talk about Latina/os (or in the lingua franca and U.S. government parlance, "Hispanics"), they are referring to a diverse population of individuals and groups. Under this rubric are included people who descend from inhabitants of Mexico, countries of Central and South America, and the Spanish-speaking Caribbean. Most of this population is composed of people of Mexican descent. Puerto Ricans[2] and Cubans are the next largest groups, followed by people from Central and South America and the Dominican Republic. Of these populations, about 21 percent of Central Americans and 67 percent of Mexicans were born in the United States, indicating a continuing influx of these populations to the United States. (See Sidebar One.)

All Latina/os experience the effects of documentation and immigration status—even citizens born in this country encounter people who stereotype them as immigrants and treat them accordingly. For those not born in this country, their status with the U.S. government affects their access to social services such as health and education, and can provoke worries that they and their families will be returned to their country of origin against their wishes.[3]

WHAT DO WE MEAN BY EDUCATION?

This paper focuses on kindergarten through 12th grade (K-12), with the bulk of our comments centering on public education. Given that nearly half of Latina/os aged 15 and older have less than a high school education (U.S. Census Bureau: 1998) and that more than 90 percent of Latina/o children attend public schools (U.S. Department of Education: 1998a), this focus should come as no surprise. We discuss private, parochial, and alternative schooling (such as the General Equivalency Diploma) when information is relevant. At the college level, we discuss Latinas' educational experiences in community colleges, liberal arts schools, state schools, and universities.[4]

Most teachers tend to think of attending college as the only measure of success after high school. They will often denigrate jobs in construction or fast food and look down on community or junior colleges. The message for the student who wants to be a refrigerator repairman is clear: high school is only for the college-bound. The kid doesn't see the point and starts flunking.

—Toni Falbo (Vail: 1998)

We will discuss educational success in the terms used by most experts who study education in the United States: measures such as persistence rates, grade point average (GPA), scores on standardized tests, time to degree completion, and enrollment rates in various academic tracks (remedial versus college-preparatory classes, for example). These indicators nearly universally test a school's success with only one aspect of education: the formal curriculum. Schools transmit three different types of curricula: the formal curriculum (or content-based instructional goals), the informal curriculum (or culturally dictated goals surrounding in-class behavior and attitudes that are not formalized in the curriculum), and the evaded curriculum (subjects, such as peer relations and harassment in school, avoided by most schools in their formal curriculum) (AAUW Educational Foundation: 1992). Informal and evaded curricular issues are often overlooked in, or separated from, the discourse about school achievement.

These measures also emphasize individual achievement and do not allow for conceptualization of success or failure at the group level (such as the family or community level). Yet any discussion of educational success must necessarily take into account the context in which success is defined and understood by Latinas themselves. Students from non-Anglo, non-middle-class backgrounds—many of whom are the first in their families to make it to, much less through, high school, or to consider college—often have ways of organizing their lives and defining success that are not tapped by traditional measures of achievement. For example, rather than measuring their success through individual grades or uninterrupted school enrollment, students can see themselves as part of a larger collective (a family, for example) whose overall success is compromised by individualized definitions of achievement or success. If success were measured at the family level, high school graduates who go to work may be judged successful—especially if their work ensures that other siblings will be able to persist in school. Researchers have observed that these realities and

Sidebar One: Selected Characteristics by Country of Origin							
Country of origin	Mexico	Puerto Rico	Cuba	Dominican Republic	Central America	South America	Spain
Percent of Hispanic population in the United States	**61.2**	12.1	4.8	*2.4*	6.0	4.7	4.4
Percent who hold a BA or BS degree	*6.2*	9.5	16.6	7.8	9.0	19.5	**20.5**
Percent who graduated from high school	44.2	53.4	56.8	*42.6*	45.6	70.7	**76.7**
Percent born in the United States	66.7		28.3	29.4	*21.0*	25.1	**82.6**
Percent who speak English very well	49.1	58.6	45.5	36.3	*34.5*	45.4	**68.1**
Percent of families headed by a female	*18.2*	36.6	*16.3*	**41.2**	22.6	18.0	18.0
Percent of families in poverty	23.4	29.6	11.4	**33.4**	20.9	12.0	*9.7*

Bold figures are the highest in each category; italic figures are the lowest.
Source: U.S. Census Bureau: *We the American ... Hispanics* (1993) (1990 Census)

measures of success are not acknowledged in many school contexts. We will discuss alternative formulations of success in more depth later in this paper, and we will explore the informal and evaded factors behind the numbers that measure success according to the formal curriculum.

WHAT DO WE MEAN BY "POSSIBLE SELVES"?

We use the concept of "possible selves" throughout the paper to articulate the interaction between Latinas' current social contexts and their perceived options for the present and the future. The concept "pertains to how individuals think about their potential and about their future. These possible selves are individualized or personalized, but they are also distinctly social" (Markus & Nurius: 1986, p. 964). The concept assumes that only in social interactions with others (families, peers, school personnel, media, and so forth) do individuals cultivate beliefs about "the pool of possible selves" from which they imagine and claim their place in the world. Many accounts of educational experiences, particularly for girls, focus on the concept of self-esteem. We prefer the concept of possible selves because it explicitly draws on contextual factors. It acknowledges the influence of "individuals' particular sociocultural and historical context and ... the models, images, and symbols provided by the media and ... immediate social experiences" (Markus & Nurius: 1986, p. 954).

The link between social context and the formation of possible selves is critically important to our ability to understand and explain the educational experiences of Latinas in the United States. This is especially true when we consider the extent to which possible selves are gendered: girls' images of who they can and should be differ from those of boys. For example, pregnancy, housework, and stereotypes of "women's work" and career options have an impact on girls' possible selves in ways that differ from boys' possible selves. Conversely, cultural ideals about masculinity will affect how boys envision their present and future possibilities and their level of academic engagement or identification.

Other social characteristics such as class, religion, and residential patterns (rural, suburban, or urban) also affect the formation of possible selves. For children whose families' values are congruent with those of the school and other community members, maturation leads to a gradual confluence of possible selves. Educational aspirations and priorities, in other words, mesh with those envisioned by family and community. Furthermore, middle-class Anglo students generally have access to resources that make a variety of current and potential possible selves seem like realistic ambitions. An affluent suburban Anglo girl with parents in the professions will have a very different sense of her future than a Mexican girl whose whole family works in the fields in rural California and whose parents have a fourth-grade education. The latter girl may find that the assumptions of the educational system conflict with other aspects of her identity (within her family, peer group, and community) and other possible selves. The difference may not be in what the girls aspire to, but in the degree to which that self seems a plausible goal: while both girls may value and aspire to college, the *perceived possibility* of it will differ markedly for the two girls.

Latinas may find that family, community, school, and peer expectations are more discordant for them than for girls of Anglo, middle-class culture. Family expectations that children, especially daughters, stay relatively close to home during and after high school conflict somewhat with a prevailing trend in middle-class culture for successful students to go away to college for four years. Similarly, the expectation that women postpone motherhood or marriage while completing an education may conflict with family or cultural norms of earlier marriage or more extensive family loyalties and commitments than is typical in Anglo, middle-class culture.

Individuals do not form possible selves with perfect knowledge or absolute power. Moreover, identity is always contested terrain—particularly for minorities whose relationship to the dominant culture has been marked by racism and ethnocentrism. The construction of a self that reflects ethnic identity is a constant struggle, particularly in contexts that attempt to de-ethnicize or subtract students' identities—for example, in schools that devalue or diminish rather than build on and nurture their students' resources in the family or community (Valenzuela: 1999). A multitude of possible selves —from school girl to family member—may be fraught with confusion and conflict. Conversely, this multitude may provide a fluidity and flexibility that allow a young woman to maintain comfortable relationships in a variety of settings that would otherwise seem contradictory—what Chicana feminist scholar and activist Gloria Anzaldúa characterizes as a dual, "mestiza" consciousness (Anzaldúa: 1987).

PART 1: OVERVIEW OF TRENDS OF LATINAS' EDUCATIONAL PARTICIPATION

We are wary of several trends in the literature about the measures of achievement reviewed in this section. First, the terminology used is highly charged, and can have negative effects on policy as well as on children themselves, who are not immune to adult descriptions of their behavior. For instance, do we refer to "dropout rates" (which focus on the failure of the group) or to "graduation rates" (which focus on the success of the group)? Researchers have devised terms other than "dropping out" to emphasize the role of institutions and schools: in addition to leaving, students are at risk of being "pushed out" by schools (Fine: 1991), or "getting out" of bad educational environments (Muñoz: 1995).

A similar dilemma characterizes our second major group of indicators of educational participation: program-taking. Researchers and policy makers tend to focus on what percentage of students enroll in college-preparatory, general education, special education, gifted and talented, or remedial courses in high school. On the postsecondary level, research focuses on college selection—two-year or four-year, and private or public—and persistence rates. Researchers' language can make course-taking and college enrollment and selection appear guided by the discretion of the student alone, and can gloss over the critical role that institutional practices, chiefly through tracking, play in the process. Therefore, we will discuss tracking at some length to call attention to the impact that schools (through counselors, teachers, and their interpretation of standardized test scores) have on the choices students perceive to be available. These data may be more reflective of persistent school trends than of individual choice.

GRADUATION RATES

One of the most commonly cited measures of a group's educational progress is its high school graduation rate. Unfortunately, this measure is complicated by a number of factors,[5] and comparison from one study to another can result in confusion and different conclusions. If we consider only those students who ever enrolled in a U.S. school, about 80 percent have a diploma or GED (Secada et al.: 1998). On the other hand, according to the most recent U.S. Department of Education data, nearly one in three (30 percent) of the nation's Latina/o students between the ages of 16 and 24 left school without either a high school diploma or an alternative certificate such as a GED, and only about half of Latina/os overall between the ages of 16 and 24 have a high school diploma (U.S. Census Bureau: 1998). The Hispanic dropout rate is only 4 percent lower than when national dropout data for Hispanics were first collected in 1972, and higher than it was 20 years ago, the Department of Education reports. Latina/o students are at greater risk of not finishing school than any other ethno-racial group and tend to leave school at an earlier age than members of any other group (Secada et al.: 1998; Hispanic Children: 1985).

Status dropout rates—or the overall percentage of 16- to 24-year-olds without a diploma—have not decreased over the past 25 years (Adelman: 1999; Secada et al.: 1998; AAUW Educational Foundation: 1998) for Latinas or Latinos. According to the Department of Education, "This may be due, in part, to high dropout rates for Hispanics before 10th grade, and high immigration rates for less educated Hispanic young adults who may never enter U.S. schools" (U.S. Department of Education: 1995, p. 6). Economic exigencies also appear to affect the dropout rate, which peaks at the age when the student can legally work (Rodríguez: 2000).

Gender and Graduation Rates

The graduation rate for Latinas is lower than for girls in any other racial or ethnic group. In 1993, 8 percent of Latinas dropped out, compared with 5 percent of African American girls and 4 percent of White girls (Phillips: 1998). Most groups of girls have lower dropout rates than their male peers, although data vary by year and region.

Compared to Latinos, persistence rates for Latinas are roughly equal, although girls have a slightly higher chance of finishing 12 years of schooling than boys (AAUW Educational Foundation: 1998). Interestingly, girls actually have lower persistence rates between 9th and 12th grade than boys—probably because boys leave school earlier than girls, so that those boys who remain into high school are more likely to stay (Hernández: 1995). In the San Diego school system, for example, almost half—48 percent—of public school dropouts in 1998 were Latina/o, with males comprising 26 percent of these dropouts, and females, 22 percent. Latina/os are 36 percent of the school population, yet account for 48 percent of 1998 dropouts (San Diego City Schools: 2000). In the southwestern states of Colorado, Arizona, California, New Mexico, and Texas, 38 percent of Mexican women and 37 percent of Mexican men 25 years or older have completed eight years or less of education; 21 percent of women and 19 percent of men have completed four years of high school; and 5 percent of women and 7 percent of men have completed four or more years of college. In contrast, 21 percent of Anglo women, 31 percent of Asian women, and 14 percent of African American women in the same region have completed four or more years of college (U.S. Census Bureau: 1993a).

Girls who do leave school are less likely than their male counterparts to return and complete school. As researcher Lynn Phillips notes, "Once [B]lack and Hispanic girls leave school, they are less likely than [B]lack and Hispanic boys to make up their educational loss" (AAUW Educational Foundation: 1998; Phillips: 1998, p. 68).

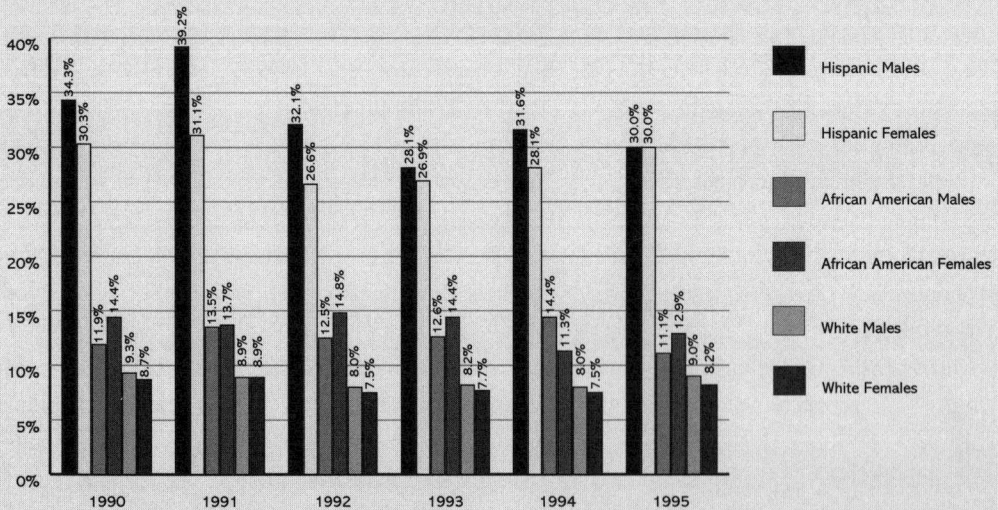

Percent of High School Dropouts Among Persons 16-24 Years Old, by Sex and Race/Ethnicity, 1990-1995

Source: U.S. Department of Commerce, Bureau of the Census, Current Population Reports, 2000

Country of Origin and Generational Status

These factors are also correlated with high school graduation rates. Another way of getting at this trend is to consider data from areas with relatively high concentrations of immigrants from a given country. For example, in Miami—an area with a large Cuban community—the dropout rate of Latina/os is about equal to that of Anglos, as it is in San Antonio with its large and well-established Mexican-American community. In other areas, it is as much as three times as high as the dropout rate for Anglos (Rendón & Amaury: 1987).

Status dropout rates (cumulative data on all Latina/o 16- to 24-year-olds, regardless of their most recent attendance) are also related to generational status. The U.S. Department of Education reports the following percentages of Latina/os did not receive a diploma by the age of 24 (U.S. Department of Education: 1995):
- 43 percent of those who were foreign-born (over half of whom never enrolled in a U.S. school)
- 21 percent of first generation
- 24 percent of second generation or more

Yet in some respects, the dropout rate transcends generational lines. Dropout rates for Hispanics are higher than for non-Hispanics of similar immigration and generational status, according to national data. Hispanic dropout rates were lower for those with U.S.-born parents, yet still double those of non-Hispanics of comparable residency status. Hence, high status dropout rates "are not just a problem associated with recent immigration" (U.S. Department of Education: 1995, p. 7). Whereas 2 percent of second-generation Asians had never completed high school nor were working toward this goal, 12 percent of their Hispanic counterparts matched this description (U.S. Department of Education: 1998a).

SUSPENSIONS

School suspensions are generally considered to have a relationship to dropping out. Nationwide, Hispanics account for 14 percent of school suspensions, which corresponds roughly to their representation in the school population. However, Hispanic males are much more likely to be suspended than Hispanic females (10 percent to 4 percent) and account for more suspensions (10 percent of students suspended) than their representation in the school population (7 percent of total students). On a statewide level, Latinos in Texas comprise 19 percent of school population, but 29 percent of school suspensions—almost 50 percent higher than their representation in the school population. White males in Texas, by contrast, comprise 23 percent of the school population and roughly the same percentage—24 percent—of suspensions. In Florida the number of Latinos suspended (9 percent of all students suspended) mirrors their number in the population (9 percent of students) (Office for Civil Rights: 1999).

Latinas, in turn, while suspended less than their male peers, are suspended at a higher rate than White or Asian girls, although in many states less frequently than African American girls.[6] Latinas in Texas comprise 18 percent of the school population and contribute 11 percent of the suspensions—almost 50 percent lower than their representation in the school. White females are suspended at an even lower rate than Latinas: they make up 22 percent of the school population and only 7 percent of suspensions, almost 70 percent lower than their representation in school. Similar, although less pronounced, differences are evident in California, Arizona, and New Mexico (Office for Civil Rights: 1999).

TRACKING AND COURSE-TAKING

Course- and program-taking is another major indicator of academic success used by institutions, especially the rate at which students are enrolled in college-preparatory educational tracks. As we have suggested, a student's ability to enroll in a particular academic program is highly influenced by formal and informal tracking in the school. Tracking, which can begin in middle school, is based on teacher and counselor recommendations and on standardized test scores. This practice, and other institutional characteristics such as course availability, shapes students' program-taking (Oakes: 1990). The practice of tracking students by ability or educational need emerged initially as an idea promising to tailor education to the needs of individual students. Subsequent research has shown, however, that tracking may have adverse effects on *all* students—even those in the accelerated programs (Oakes: 1990). The effects of tracking may be particularly complex for language-minority students, many of whom have great intellectual capacity, but are hindered by their ability to understand verbal or written English.

Despite the prevalence of tracking practices in public schools, Latina/os may not have much knowledge or "cultural capital" with which to navigate and understand the tracking process in high school. Relative to Asian 8th graders, Hispanics are more likely to respond that they do not know what kind of high school program they intend to enroll in (32 percent). Asian 8th graders are more likely to plan to enroll in a college preparatory program in high school than their Hispanic peers (36 percent to 22 percent) (U.S. Department of Education: 1998a).

College Preparatory Programs

Roughly 70 percent of Latina/o high school students are enrolled in classes that will **not** prepare them for college (Hispanic Children: 1985; Adelman: 1999), although estimates vary. In addition, although Latina/o students are taking more credit hours of classes in high school than in the past, they are less likely than their Anglo counterparts to have taken a core curriculum of four units of English and three units each of science, social studies, and mathematics (U.S. Department of Education: 1995). In 1992, Hispanics were less likely than White graduates to have taken geometry, Algebra II, chemistry, trigonometry, physics, or a combination of biology, chemistry, and physics; they were more likely to have taken remedial mathematics (U.S. Department of Education: 1995). Course-taking patterns differ among college-bound students as well: the College Board reports that in 1999 Whites reported the most year-long academic courses (19.6) and Mexican Americans the least (18.1) (College Board: 1999a).

Differences in mathematics course-taking–especially advanced classes and Algebra II—are particularly troubling and noteworthy, since several pieces of research based on national data have suggested that the completion of Algebra I and geometry early in high school is a major predictor of college enrollment (Kane & Pelavin: 1990; Adelman: 1999) and may be particularly important for Latina/o students (Perna: 2000). It is unclear whether the lower mathematics and science course-taking for Latina/os differs between males and females, although prior observed sex differences in mathematics and science enrollment overall call for further research and data to explore Latina and Latino course-taking patterns.

Themes and Questions for Further Research:
- Do Latina and Latino course- or program-taking in K-12 differ? If so, how and why?
- How does Latina persistence change from K-16+? Is there a pattern of higher persistence up to high school and decreased persistence thereafter relative to Latinos and to other women? If so, why?

Special Education

There is evidence that Latina/o students are being tracked disproportionately—and perhaps erroneously—into special education programs. According to the Department of Education, between 1976 and 1994 Hispanics with learning disabilities increased from 24 percent to 51 percent of all students with learning disabilities (President's Advisory Commission: 1996). Substantial numbers of Latina/o children, with and without English proficiency, are being classified as "seriously emotionally disturbed" (SED) or "specific learning disabled" (SLD). Gender also conditions this labeling process. Overall, as 1992 research by the AAUW Educational Foundation notes, males outnumber females in special education programs by "startling percentages"—particularly in the population of students given the most subjective diagnosis of "emotionally disturbed" (AAUW Educational Foundation: 1992, p. 29).

National data on Latina/os identified as SED or SLD reveal that Hispanic males are indeed more likely to be referred for special education than Latinas. Yet compared to their White and African American male peers, Latinos are somewhat less likely to be diagnosed as SED. Nationwide, Hispanic males contribute the same percentage of students diagnosed as SED as their overall representation in the school population (7 percent), and Asian males contribute fewer. White and African American males are more likely to be diagnosed as SED or SLD relative to their representation in the school population (Office for Civil Rights: 1999).

Conversely, females are generally underrepresented in the SED and SLD categories. Latinas comprise 7 percent of the school population, yet only 2 percent of those students diagnosed as SED. Latinos were over three times more likely to be diagnosed as SED and two times more likely to be diagnosed as SLD than Latinas, which generally mirrors the pattern for White students (Office for Civil Rights: 1999).

Examination of SED and SLD data from California and Texas provides additional evidence of the underrepresentation of all but African American girls relative to their population in the school. The pattern among boys differs somewhat from the national data in that Latinos contribute less than their proportion in the population to SED and SLD placements while at the national level they were assigned in proportion to their numbers (Office for Civil Rights: 1999).

Examination of data on special education cases by race/ethnicity and sex provokes important questions about tracking and diagnosis. If socioeconomic, cultural, and environmental factors explain different rates of diagnosis between groups, one would expect to see less variation *within* racial/ethnic categories between males and females. If, on the other hand, male students are developmentally more prone toward learning and behavioral problems or disadvantaged by teaching or learning styles in the classroom, one would expect to see less variation across racial/ethnic groups in rates of male and female diagnoses. The inherently subjective nature of special education diagnoses, and the sex and racial/ethnic differences evident here, should alert us to the possibility that different expectations and norms for males and females may be leading some groups (Latinas, for example) to be underidentified and other groups (African American and White males, for example) to be overidentified. In any case, differences by race/ethnicity and sex at the state and national levels in SED and SLD diagnoses require further research and explanation.

Gifted and Talented Education

Hispanics generally are underrepresented in Gifted and Talented Education (GATE) programs relative to their representation in the school population and in comparison to their White and Asian American peers. Hispanics are 14 percent of students nationwide, for example, and 8 percent of the GATE students (4 percent male; 4 percent female). In California, they are 40 percent of students overall, and 22 percent of GATE students; in Texas, they are 37 percent of students and 26 percent of GATE students; in Arizona, they are 28 percent of students and 11 percent of GATE students; in New Mexico they are 49 percent of students and 25 percent of GATE students; and in New York, they are 18 percent of students and only 4 percent of GATE students. In Florida, GATE enrollment more closely parallels overall Hispanic enrollment (16 percent of students; 14 percent of GATE students) (Office for Civil Rights: 1999).

Although Latinas and Latinos differ in their representation in special education for SED or SLD, they have roughly similar enrollments to one another in GATE programs nationwide and in states such as California, Florida, Texas, Arizona, New York, and New Mexico. Compared with their female peers, Latinas are underenrolled in GATE courses. Whereas White and Asian females constitute higher percentages of the GATE population than their representation in the school population overall (31 percent of school population, 39 percent of GATE students; 2 percent of school population, 4 percent of GATE students, respectively), Latinas constitute a lower percentage (7 percent of population; 4 percent of GATE students). African American females are also underrepresented, by half, in GATE programs (8 percent of school population; 4 percent of GATE students) (Office for Civil Rights: 1999).

Themes and Questions for Further Research:
- What accounts for differences by sex and race/ethnicity in special education programs and in gifted and talented programs on a national and state-by-state level?

Enrollment in Advanced Placement Courses and Exam-Taking

AP Course-taking. Latina/o students are underrepresented in challenging Advanced Placement (AP) courses that allow students to earn college credit for high school work in several subject areas. Relative to their representation in schools, Latinas are less likely to enroll in AP Mathematics or Science than their White and Asian peers. White and Asian girls overenroll in AP Mathematics and Science, relative to their representation in the school population nationwide (31 percent of students; 35 percent of AP Math students; 2 percent of students, 6 percent of AP Math students, respectively). Latinas and African American girls underenroll by almost half (Office for Civil Rights: 1999). Their underrepresentation undoubtedly reflects in large part the lack of AP course availability in many predominantly Latina/o and African American schools (Clewell & Braddock: 2000). The Tomás Rivera Policy Institute in California finds sharp discrepancies in AP course availability among California public high schools. In large school districts, 62 percent of schools that offer no AP courses are predominantly Latina/o and African American, and overall, 15 percent of the public schools offer no AP courses. The Institute notes that the University of California campuses rank the number of AP courses and performance in them as the fourth criteria for selecting prospective students, so that students who are not given an opportunity to pursue these intensive courses are at a disadvantage (Tomás Rivera Policy Institute: 1999).

Nationwide and in key states such as California, Texas, Florida, New Mexico, Arizona, and New York, similar percentages of Hispanic males and females take AP Mathematics and AP Science courses, yet their numbers overall are not strong. Hispanics are 7 percent of both AP Math and Science course-takers, evenly distributed between males and females, which is half of their overall school enrollment of 14 percent. The numbers are lower in Arizona (29 percent of students; 9 percent of AP Math and 11 percent of AP Science course-takers); California (40 percent of students; 16 percent of AP Math and 13 percent of AP Science course-takers); and, especially, New York (18 percent of students; 2 percent each of AP Math and Science course-takers). The numbers are more positive, but still disproportionately low, in Texas, where Hispanics are 37 percent of students, 22 percent of AP Math and 20 percent of AP Science course-takers, and the most positive in Florida (16 percent of students; 10 percent of AP Math and 11 percent of AP Science course-takers) (Office for Civil Rights: 1999).

Although few Hispanics overall take AP Computer Science courses, more males than females do so. In some states, as few as six Latinas and 19 Latinos (Arizona), eight Latinas and 36 Latinos (Florida), and three Latinas and 20 Latinos (New York) take AP Computer Science courses. The exceptions are California and Texas, where in contrast to the gender gap for White students, roughly equal numbers of Hispanic males and females take AP Computer Science courses (Office for Civil Rights: 1999).

Again, these numbers—especially in states with concentrated Hispanic school districts—undoubtedly reflect the availability of challenging courses, lack of resources for teaching, and formal or informal tracking practices, rather than disinterest on the part of individual students.

AP Test-taking and Scores. Generally, Latinas take the same number of or more AP exams than their male counterparts, especially in the language arts, yet they take fewer AP exams than White and Asian girls. Latinas outnumber Latinos in English literature (65 percent of Hispanic test-takers), English composition (63 percent of Hispanic test-takers), Spanish language (57 percent of Hispanic test-takers), and Spanish literature (68 percent of Hispanic test-takers). Latinas, in fact, comprise nearly half (47 percent) of all of the Spanish literature exam-takers in the country and 70 percent of the female exam-takers. Latinos, in contrast, are 22 percent of all Spanish literature exam-takers. Latinas, apparently, have been encouraged to pursue advanced language and literature courses, or have found ways to engage in these areas of the curriculum. In several areas, such as European and U.S. history, Latina and Latino test-taking is roughly comparable (College Board: 1999).

Latina/o test-taking mirrors the overall gender gap in mathematics and science AP exams in some areas but is less pronounced in others. More Hispanic males than females took the AP exam in chemistry (59 percent of Hispanic test-takers), calculus (60 percent of Hispanic test-takers), physics (65 percent of Hispanic test-takers), computer science (83 percent of Hispanic test-takers), and economics-micro (57 percent of Hispanic test-takers). Although overall, more males than females take statistics and Calculus AB, Latinas were as likely as Latinos to take these exams; yet in general, very few Latina/os took them (College Board: 1999).

Latinas' AP test-taking is lower as a percentage of the population than that of any other group of girls, as is Latino test-taking vis-á-vis other groups of students.

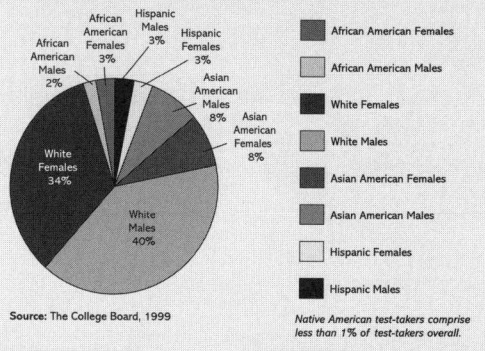

Calculus AB Advanced Placement Test-Takers, by Sex and Race/Ethnicity, 1999*

Source: The College Board, 1999

Native American test-takers comprise less than 1% of test-takers overall.

*Includes only those students who recorded their race/ethnicity, and excludes those who "did not state" their race or recorded "other."

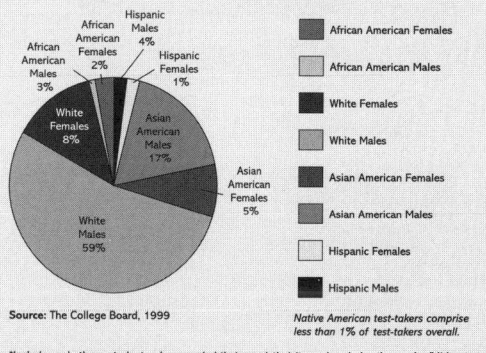

Computer Science A Advanced Placement Test-Takers, by Sex and Race/Ethnicity, 1999*

Source: The College Board, 1999

Native American test-takers comprise less than 1% of test-takers overall.

*Includes only those students who recorded their race/ethnicity, and excludes those who "did not state" their race or recorded "other."

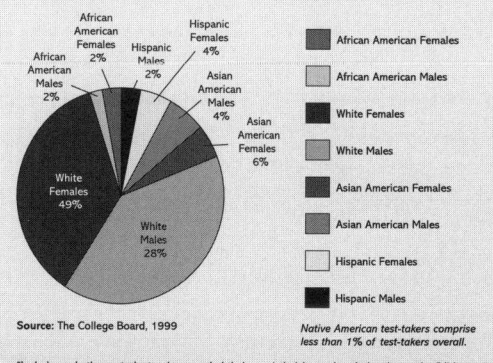

English Literature & Composition Advanced Placement Test-Takers, by Sex and Race/Ethnicity, 1999*

Source: The College Board, 1999

Native American test-takers comprise less than 1% of test-takers overall.

*Includes only those students who recorded their race/ethnicity, and excludes those who "did not state" their race or recorded "other."

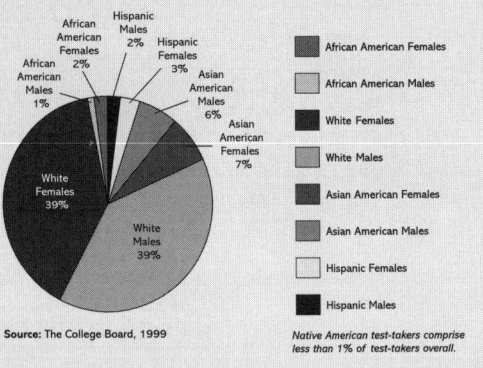

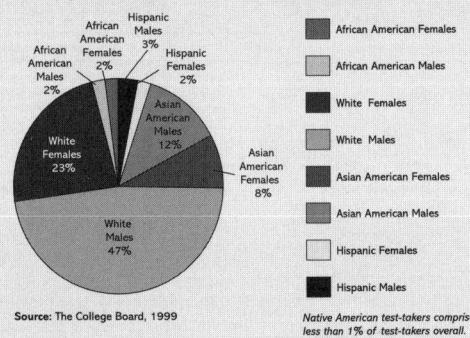

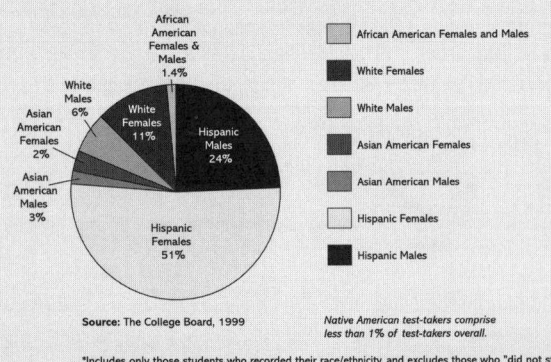

Furthermore, in many subject areas Latina/os score more credit-ineligible grades of "1" or "2" than White students. Latinas comprise roughly 2 to 3 percent of female test-takers on most subject exams, although their representation in the female U.S. population is closer to 7 percent, and higher in the school-age population. In many areas, the number of Latina or Latino test-takers could easily be accommodated in one large room: only 317 Latinas took the economics-micro exam (185 Mexican Americans, 28 Puerto Ricans, and 104 "Other Hispanic"), 436 took the physics exam, 375 took the Calculus AB exam, and, although 28,185 women overall took the European History AP exam, only 1,472 of them were Latina (College Board: 1999).

Latinas' AP exam-taking is lowest—and the gender gap most noticeable—on the computer science exams. Only 127 Latinas in the country took the Computer Science A exam, compared to 406 Latinos (76 percent of the Hispanic test-takers). No Puerto Rican woman—and only 16 Latinas overall—took the more extensive Computer Science AB exam. In 1999, 11,793 students took the Computer Science A exam, with Latinas comprising less than 1 percent of the test-takers (College Board: 1999).

Differences among Hispanic test-takers illustrate the diversity among populations of Latinos. Although Mexican Americans make up a larger share of the Hispanic population (65 percent of total), they comprise a lower percentage of AP test-takers. Those who identified as "Other Hispanic"—Cuban American or Central American, for example—comprise a higher share of test-takers. Puerto Rican participation is low across all subject areas, and in some cases (i.e., physics, economics, government and politics, composition), fewer than 100 students nationwide participate (College Board: 1999).

STANDARDIZED TEST SCORES

To make statements about the educational achievement of all students in the United States, children regularly take standardized as well as curriculum-based tests. Standardized tests measure competency with reading, math, and language skills, without regard for the curriculum taught in a given classroom or school. In recent years several states with large Latina/o populations, including Texas, have instituted standardized testing to measure student and school performance at the state and district level.[7] The National Assessment of Educational Progress (NAEP) exam is a nationally representative, although voluntary, exam administered to 4th, 8th, and 12th graders to measure knowledge in specific subject areas. The Scholastic Aptitude Test (SAT) is a high stakes exam for high school juniors and seniors, and most colleges and scholarship competitions use it as one selection criterion. This competitive test is often perceived as a college gatekeeper.

NAEP Scores

Although improving, the achievement gap between Hispanic and White 13-year-olds remains daunting, especially in mathematics and science. According to the U.S. Department of Education, "Hispanic children's level of math skills may be as much as two years behind that of their White peers by the age of 13—a deficiency that they will carry with them into high school" (U.S. Department of Education: 1995).

The gender gap in NAEP test scores is larger for Hispanics than for White students and favors Latinas in several subject areas—a pattern also found among African American students (AAUW Educational Foundation: 1998).

In the 4th grade, Latinas score higher than Latinos in reading and history; by the 8th grade, they score higher in mathematics and reading; and by the 12th grade, they score higher than Latinos in science as well as reading. The achievement gap between White girls and boys is smaller at each assessment point, with girls outscoring boys only on reading in the 4th and 12th grades.

SAT Scores

Latinas outnumber their male counterparts in taking the SAT exam (58 percent to 42 percent in 1999), yet they score lower than their male counterparts on both the math and verbal sections. Latinas are less likely to take the exam than their White or Asian American counterparts, and those who do score lower on average than those groups of girls.

The mean verbal SAT score for Mexican American girls was 448—76 points lower than the mean score for White girls (524); Latin American girls scored a mean of 457—67 points lower than the mean for White girls. On the math section, Mexican American girls scored a mean of 441 and Latin American girls, 446—71 and 66 points lower, respectively, than the mean score for White girls (College Board: 1999a).

Hispanic males score higher than females on the verbal section of the SAT, and higher still on the math section. Mexican American males scored 11 points higher than females on the verbal test and 35 points higher on the math; Latin American males scored 14 points higher on the verbal and 42 points higher on the math (College Board: 1999a).

The gender gap on both math and verbal scores between all Hispanic test-takers is larger than that between White, African American, Native American, and Asian test-takers. Mean scores of White and Asian males and females on the verbal section, for example, differ by seven points (College Board: 1999a).

GRADES

As with the other individual measures, Latina/os in grades K-12 tend to have lower grades than their classmates, even after controlling for social class and other related variables. Grades are correlated with both gender and generational status. On average,

Latinas have higher grades than Latinos in 9th grade (Adams, Astone, & Nunez-Wormack: 1994) and college (Rumberger & Larson: 1998), and new immigrants have higher GPAs in 9th grade than children or grandchildren of immigrants (Adams et al.: 1994). In a study that controlled for tracking, however, this generational pattern was observed only if students were located in the lower track. No statistical differences were observed if students were located in the upper track (i.e., honors, college bound, or magnet programs) (Valenzuela: 1999). Grades may be an important factor in understanding lack of persistence: in one study of boys and girls, only 8 percent of graduates had grades below C, while 54 percent of those who dropped out had low grades (Valverde: 1987).

COLLEGE ENROLLMENT BY TYPE OF COLLEGE

Other common measures of achievement used in the United States are whether or not an individual goes to college and whether he or she enters a vocational school, community college, four-year college, or university. In 1992, Latina/os who graduated from high school were as likely as other graduates to pursue higher education (about 60 percent continue after high school), although the type of college entered differed (U.S. Department of Education: 1995). However, among college-aspiring students in their sophomore year of high school, a smaller percentage actually enrolls in a four-year institution immediately after graduation (37 percent of Hispanics in comparison with 56 percent of Whites, 55 percent of Asian Americans, and 39 percent of African Americans) (Perna: 2000).

Although Latina/os who graduated from high school are making the transition to college at about the same rate as Anglos, they are concentrated in community colleges (Darden, Bagakás, & Armstrong: 1994). In 1996 a substantial majority—69 percent—of all Hispanic students (including those in graduate and professional schools) attended two-year public or private institutions. The largest number—54 percent—attended public two-year institutions. To the extent that they are represented in four-year schools, they more often attend state institutions; few attend private institutions or research universities. Thirty-one percent attended four-year public institutions, while only 2 percent attended four-year private institutions (this number includes students pursuing doctoral or professional degrees, so the number of *undergraduates* attending private four-year institutions is undoubtedly smaller still). Hispanics are also clustered in specific institutions: one-third of Hispanic students in higher education are enrolled in only 189 of the 3,000 two- and four-year institutions in the United States (President's Advisory Commission: 1996).

Although data are unavailable to discern whether Hispanic males and females attend different types of institutions at different rates, Latinas do comprise a higher percentage of associate's degree recipients and thus are probably well-represented at two-year and community colleges that focus on associate's programs (U.S. Department of Education: 2000).

Among undergraduates, barely half of Hispanics enrolled in 1996 attended school full time. Men were more likely to attend school full-time than women (U.S. Department of Education: 1996a).

COMPLETION OF DEGREES

Latinas outnumber Latinos in completion of the associate's (59 percent to 41 percent), bachelor's (52 percent to 48 percent), and master's (52 percent to 48 percent) degrees. Latinos outnumber Latinas in their completion of professional degrees (56 percent to 44 percent) and doctorates (51 percent to 49 percent). Hispanics overall are dramatically underrepresented among doctoral recipients: of the 44,652 doctorates conferred in 1996, Latinas received 462 (1 percent of total) and Latinos 488 (1 percent of total). These percentages, according to a federal report, have "remained relatively flat since the 1980s." Latinas are the least likely of any group of women in the U.S. to complete a bachelor's degree (President's Advisory Commission:

1996, p. 5; U.S. Department of Education: 2000; U.S. Department of Education: 1998a).

In postsecondary education, the national persistence rate for all Latinas is between 60 and 75 percent (Ginorio, Gutiérrez, Cauce, & Acosta: 1995), although this figure varies significantly from institution to institution. Even at Hispanic-serving institutions, noncompletion rates can be staggering. At New Mexico Highlands University, for example, only 5 percent of a given entering class will graduate in four years; only 30 percent have graduated after 10 years (Cornwell: 1998).

MAJORS

Latinas constitute a higher percentage of education associate's degrees than White women and earn far more of these degrees (76 percent of Hispanic education majors) than their male counterparts. At the associate's and bachelor's level, Latinas are less likely than White women to earn degrees in health sciences but far more likely than Latinos to earn degrees in this field: three-fourths of health science associate's degrees for Hispanics are earned by women (U.S. Department of Education: 1995; U.S Department of Education: 1998a).

Bachelor's Degrees: Subject Areas

Just as Latina/os tend to be clustered in particular schools, the majority pursue only a few majors. The most common bachelor's degree majors for Latina/os mirror those of the overall bachelor's degree population. Business management draws almost 20 percent of Latina/o undergraduates (10,765), half of whom are Latina. The social sciences and history also attract roughly equal numbers of Latinas and Latinos, and represent 7,155 of Hispanic bachelor's degrees. As with bachelor's recipients overall, Latinas are much more likely to receive a bachelor's in education—a popular major—than their male counterparts (2,865 to 871 or 77 percent of Hispanic bachelor's in education). Similarly, Latinas outnumber their male counterparts in psychology (3,345 to 1,186 or 74 percent of Hispanic psychology degrees). Other popular majors in which Latinas outnumber Latinos include English (1,448 to 727), foreign languages (1,485 to 584), the health professions (2,213 to 637), liberal arts/general studies (1,651 to 721), and multi/interdisciplinary studies (1,617 to 510). Latinos outnumber Latinas in very few of the most popular majors, most notably in engineering, where 5 percent (2,811) of Hispanic undergraduates receive bachelor's degrees, 79 percent of which go to men (2,232 to 579) (U.S. Department of Education: 1998a).

Doctoral Degrees: Subject Areas

As noted earlier, there were only 950 Hispanic doctoral recipients in 1996 in the United States—488 men and 462 women. The largest percentage (209 or 22 percent) of these doctorates went to education majors, mostly Latina, which account for fully one in four (27 percent) of the Latina doctorates. Psychology is the second most popular doctorate for Latina/os, and is also disproportionately earned by Latinas (142 total: 99 Latinas and 43 Latinos). Other disciplines with at least 60 Latina/o doctoral recipients feature more males than females and include biological sciences (96 total, 52 males), social sciences and history (89 total, 55 males), engineering (83 total, 67 males), and the physical sciences (63 total, 54 males). Only one Latina in the United States (and only eight Latinos) received a doctoral degree in computer and information sciences in 1996 (U.S. Department of Education: 1998a).

Science and Engineering Participation

A National Science Foundation report identifies troubling trends in science and engineering (S&E) preparation. The majority of S&E workers are non-Hispanic White males, yet this population is projected to decline as a fraction of the workforce population from 37 percent to 26 percent by 2050. Meanwhile, groups currently underrepresented in the S&E workforce—Hispanics and African Americans—are likely to grow as a fraction of the workforce. Given these trends, Latina participation in science and engineering is especially noteworthy. The National Science Foundation reports that although Latinas comprise 6 percent of the population, they received only 3 percent of the S&E bachelor's degrees and made up only 2 percent of graduate school enrollment. At the end of the S&E pipeline, Latinas comprise less than 1 percent of the S&E workforce. Significantly, although their participation is also quite low, Latinos' participation declines less precipitously from the bachelor's to graduate to workforce level, and they contribute a higher percentage than Latinas to the S&E workforce (National Science and Technology Council: 2000).

LATINA/O FACULTY

Latinas attending colleges and universities are not likely to encounter Latinas on the faculty. In the fall of 1995, Hispanics overall comprised 12,942 of the full-time faculty members in United States colleges and universities—just 2 percent of all full-time United States faculty. Latinas comprise 5,078 of the full-time faculty (1 percent), and Latinos, 7,864. Nationwide, Latinas occupy a fraction (0.3 percent) of full professor positions: 558 Latinas occupy this rank, in comparison to 1,912 Hispanic males. The largest number and percentage of Latinas (1,668 or 33 percent) occupy the assistant professor rank, whereas almost equal numbers of Hispanic males occupy the assistant and the full professor rank (2,068 and 1,912, respectively) (U.S. Department of Education: 2000).

ECONOMIC EFFECTS OF EDUCATION

Latinas get more of an economic "return" on postsecondary education than Hispanic males, although both sexes earn more as they acquire more education.

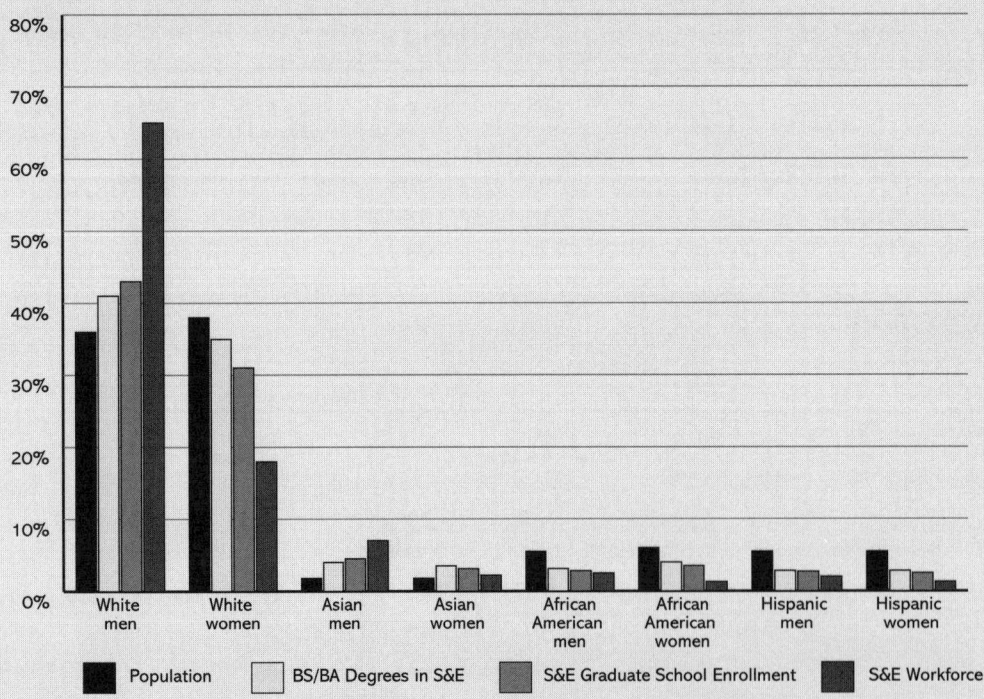

Percent of Population, Science & Engineering Degrees Awarded, Science & Engineering Graduate School Enrollment, and Science & Engineering Labor Force

Source: National Science and Technology Council, 2000

Latinas with a bachelor's degree earned 82 percent more than those with a high school diploma, while Hispanic males with a bachelor's degree earned 60 percent more. Currently, Latinas are disproportionately represented in service occupations (24 percent of Latinas; 17 percent of non-Hispanic women) and in administrative support and sales occupations. The Department of Labor attributes this trend to the fact that little more than half of employed Latina women have high school diplomas and few have college degrees. Latinas' labor force participation is lower than that of White women (56 percent to 60 percent); however, it is projected to increase to 80 percent by 2005. Educational opportunities, linked to substantially higher earnings for Latinas, would undoubtedly boost Latinas' share of managerial and professional positions (U.S. Department of Education: 1995; U.S. Census Bureau: 1993b; President's Advisory Commission: 1996).

PART 2: CHARACTERISTICS OF COMMUNITIES AFFECTING PARTICIPATION/SUCCESS

The remainder of this paper will explore and discuss some of the factors that contribute to the educational trends just presented and to Latinas' formation of possible selves. In this section we approach families, peer groups, and schools—both K-12 and postsecondary—as forms of community, each of which contributes to an individual's perception of future outcomes and opportunities. We cannot stress strongly enough the interaction among the factors discussed in all of the sections to follow. Any one characteristic is nearly meaningless without simultaneously considering all the elements of Latinas' lives. "Socialization can be fully understood only by examining the role of parents in light of the influence of other settings in which children and families function" (Collins, Maccoby, Steinberg, Hetherington, & Bornstein: 2000, p. 228).

For many Americans, particularly middle-class Anglos, the communities of family, peer groups, and school reinforce shared social values and agendas. The behaviors and expectations rewarded in the home are largely congruent with those rewarded in school and articulated among peers. In this sense, these communities echo and reinforce one another. For many other young people, especially people of color, messages sent by these various communities can conflict with one another. In school, this can result in a "subtractive education" (Valenzuela: 1999) that leads to increasingly bifurcated worlds: academic versus family, culture of origin versus culture of choice/identification, individualist versus community-focused values, and so on. In the ideal community, families find support for their belief systems and lifestyles from their neighbors and other social institutions. In cases where conflicts and differences exist among the values of the school, families, and communities, children may face multiple, conflicting views of who they can and should be. Schools and other institutions can approach these differences in a way that is affirming of a Latina's culture and that encourages individual academic identification and personal creativity or in a way that exacerbates a student's sense of alienation or fragmentation by dismissing the student's values.

FAMILY

A Latina will form the first images of who she can be and what should be considered realistic and rewarding options for her future self within her family of origin. A young girl's sense of possible selves benefits from a family environment that supports an array of educational and career options. Latino families are also shaped by their connections to other cultures in the United States and often characterized by marginal economic survival, segregation in poor urban neighborhoods, and an uneasy distrust of a dominant culture that is often typified by racism and intolerance. In many cases, the local school system may embody or represent these characteristics, which in turn shape the family's relationship to the school.

Family Structure

As is true of every group in the United States, there is no single "typical" Latino family. Family structure is diverse and covers the spectrum: two-parent families with no children or many living at home; single-parent families; and extended families with grandparents, adult siblings and their children, or family friends living in one home. In some homes, only Spanish is spoken; in others, only English. In still others, both are used.

Yet family structure is most often conceived in the research literature as simply the presence or absence of a father in the home. According to the U.S. Census Bureau, Hispanic families are more likely than non-Hispanic White families to have a female householder with no spouse present. Twenty-three percent of all Hispanic families, compared with 13 percent of non-Hispanic White families, were maintained by a female householder with no spouse present. Not only are Hispanic female-headed households more numerous, they also tend to be poorer than White female-headed households, with a median income of $12,406 compared to $17,414. Puerto Rican female householders have the lowest income of all Hispanic families in the country (U.S. Census Bureau: 1993b).

It is generally assumed that children in single-parent homes fare worse than children from two-parent homes due to reduced economic circumstances, limited supervision, and so on. However, not all research supports this assumption. Reyes and Jason (1993) found that 9th graders classified as being at high risk and low risk for dropping out of high school did not differ in their family structures; that is, students from high-risk groups were no more or less likely to come from single-parent homes.

Much less is known about additional elements of family structure, such as the impact of siblings, grandparents, or other adults in the home. We know very little about how different household configurations—aside from the one- or two-parent family—may affect achievement and education for Latinas. This omission in the research base has particular significance for understanding Latina/o education, since Latina mothers may draw on other adults—not spouses—in the home to cope with low wages and earnings potential and to alleviate economic distress (Ortiz: 1997).

Even less is known about the influence of siblings on a child's academic achievement. While many theorists suggest that decision-making about education in Latino families takes into account whole family needs so that an older child may curtail his or her own education to support the family economically or to allow younger children to succeed, this proposition is not well studied. Some evidence suggests that the effect of older siblings may be particularly powerful if they curtailed their own aspirations because of the need to leave school and work (Gándara: 1995). Anecdotal data suggest that siblings can play a crucial role by supporting one another through sharing chores and responsibilities, among other things (Ginorio & Grignon: 2000; Ginorio & Huston: 2000). Larger-scale data suggest that students who drop out are more likely to have siblings who dropped out, and students who graduated are more likely to have siblings who graduated (Valverde: 1987).

Themes and Questions for Further Research:
- What influence do different household configurations have, aside from the absence or presence of a father, on educational outcomes?
- What influence do siblings have on Latinas' educational outcomes and choices?

Centrality of Family

Two values that cut across many distinct "Hispanic" cultures are the centrality of the family and the importance of religious affiliation, most commonly, Catholicism (Ginorio, Gutierrez et al.: 1995). Thus, many Latinas' possible selves are more intrinsically tied to the family than are those of other ethnic and racial groups in the United States (see Sidebar Two).

Unsurprisingly, then, qualitative research also suggests that parental involvement, especially for low-income Latina/os, boosts educational outcomes (Delgado-Gaitán: 1991; Durán: 2000; Perna: 2000). Federal initiatives for Hispanic education have prescribed a positive focus on the family, noting that we "need to recognize that Hispanic families have social capital on which to build" (Lockwood & Secada: 2000). Yet there has been little discussion in research or policy of how the centrality of family life may affect Latinas and Latinos differently, despite the gendered nature of roles and responsibilities in most families in the United States. A 1998 report on college-bound students, for example, finds that the greatest discrepancy between Hispanic and White seniors has to do with the compatibility of students' home life with schooling. "One-third of Hispanic seniors, at a level at least 10 percent higher than Whites, worry about money problems, family obligations, a lack of a good place to study at home, and parental disinterest in their education" (College Bound Hispanics: 1998). Family care-giving obligations, especially, fall more on Latinas than on their male counterparts (Chacón, Cohen, Camarena, Gonzáles, & Strover: 1983).

A principal of a Denver high school that aggressively works to keep Hispanic students in school notes that "the Latino culture values education, but it values family above all. And when it comes to choosing between going to school and helping the family, the family will win." This principal combated the dropout rate by establishing flexible schedules so that students could accommodate work demands and family roles as well as school, including a program for pregnant and parenting Latinas to continue their education.

—(Vail: 1998)

By the same token, however, family ties and supports are a resource for Latina/os' educational achievement when schools are equipped to build on this strength in the community. They may provide powerful incentives and resources for Latinas to pursue education and to excel (Valenzuela: 1999), a theme that invites further research. Qualitative studies of high-achieving Latina women in academia confirm Gándara's 1995 findings that "family support was mentioned over and over" in their narratives of success. "Their families believed in education despite wide differences in educational backgrounds." Support from mothers was especially important, as it seems to be in families in which parents have little in the way of social capital. However, "being in school was never an excuse to shortcut family duties as daughter, wife, partner,

Sidebar Two: Home/School Cultural and Value Conflicts for Latina/os

Home	School
Nurtures dependency	Values independence
Children loved and enjoyed	Teacher seen as distant or cold
Nurtures cooperation	Values competition
Authoritarian style	Democratic style
Low-income children usually do not have preschool experiences	Expects preschool experiences
Low-income families are forced to value daily survival more than the educational needs of their children	Expects parents to value education above other values
Girls do not need to be educated as much as boys	Both sexes should be educated equally
Admonishes immodesty in girls	Physical education requires changing in front of others
Promotes ignorance of sexual matters	Advocates sex education
Achievement is for family satisfaction	Achievement is for self-satisfaction
Nonsegregated age groups	Segregated age groups
Segregated sex groups	Nonsegregated sex groups
Machismo for boys	Less sexually typed male ideal
Marianismo for girls	Less sexually typed female ideal
Some low-income families do not see the connection between school-related behaviors, such as daily school attendance, and doing well in school	School assumes that families know the types of child and family behaviors that lead to good school performance

Source: Vásquez-Nuttall & Romero-García (1989, p. 67)

mother, or caregiver. The family held very high expectations for her fulfilling family responsibilities at whatever age" (García & Associates: 1998). Similarly, the concept of family, rather than individual, success through education can lead parents to place a high value on Latina education as a means to elevate children, siblings, and other family members.

Neither my father nor my mother ever gave up trying to socialize me—"civilize" me, my mother would often say.

Throughout those years, they inculcated in me that intellectually and artistically I was as capable as my brothers. So they provided me with the best education they could afford. They made clear to me, nonetheless, that all this was being done not just to satisfy my own needs as an individual, above all I was being educated to serve the needs of the family I would one day have.

"When you educate a man," my father would often tell my younger sister and me, "you educate an individual. But when you educate a woman, you educate the whole family." ...

It wasn't unusual for Mexican fathers— almost regardless of class—to deny their daughters the advantages of formal schooling on the false premise that as women they would always be supported and protected by their husbands. The important thing was, then, my uncles perfunctorily stated, to get as successful a husband as could be found for the girls in the family. Problem solved.

My father was not quite the typical Mexican father in this respect. But even this atypical man, who has been and will continue to be one of the most influential people in my life, was subject to the social norms and pressures that made the education of woman a separate (if equal) experience.

—Lucha Corpi, "Epiphany: The Third Gift"
(Castillo-Speed: 1995)

Social Class and Cultural Capital

Contrary to popular beliefs about Hispanic communities, most parents hope that their children will excel in school; yet Latino families' economic and social contexts often preclude the realization of those dreams. One of the most pervasive difficulties with interpreting data about ethnic/racial minorities in the United States is untangling the effects of poverty from the effects of culture. By most measures, Latina/os are among the most impoverished members of the U.S. society (U.S. Census Bureau: 1993b). In areas where the Latino population is new to the country and in which English is a second (or not even spoken) language, poverty is rampant. But language is just part of the problem: even in areas where the Latino community is largely born in the U.S. and fluent in English, the poverty rate is twice as high as it is for Anglos (Aponte & Siles: 1994).

Both poverty and cultural differences—in terms of language and other values—create barriers to parents' effective mobilization of resources on their children's behalf. Conversely, cultural values can create assets—such as bilingualism and family support networks—for students in education-affirming schools. Social scientists use the term "cultural capital" to refer to resources such as familiarity with educational terms and jargon, the provision of reading materials in the home, and exposure to (European-based) cultural enrichment such as museums, literature, art, and music. Parents with little disposable income and a lack of familiarity with English (not to mention academic terminology) and American schooling procedures do not have the same levels or types of cultural capital as middle-class Anglo families. This is particularly problematic when schools assume that children come to their classrooms with these resources at their command and that parents can and will aggressively advocate on their child's behalf.

In 1995 12 percent of Hispanic children had parents whose highest educational level was college or above, compared with 38 percent of White children and 14 percent of African American children. More than one in four—27 percent—Hispanic children have parents whose highest level of education was "less than high school," a notably higher percentage than for African American children (16 percent) or for White children (4 percent) (U.S. Department of Education: 1997).

The Family Economy and Latinas' Contributions

Parents who have high educational goals for their children nonetheless may require labor contributions or economic support from their children for the family to survive. For children from poor families, economic need often results in poor attendance at all levels of the schooling process. Many Latinas contribute to their families with unpaid labor before the laws governing legal employment age allow them to contribute with a paycheck. For young women, this often means providing child care before and after school. For many, family labor often means they must miss their first classes of the day to look after children whose schools start later in the day. Paid and unpaid labor curtails a student's participation in extracurricular activities as well as time to spend studying and forming relationships with classmates.

Anecdotal evidence suggests that even young children may spend substantial time acting as translators to their non-English-speaking parents, a topic that deserves further exploration. A recent article on Latina/os in Washington, D.C., describes children who "connect [their families] to the English-speaking world." A director of community education interviewed for the article finds that "more often students lost time from school and lose time from learning. They simply do not come in, because they have to translate for their parents at the doctor's [office] or social services or somewhere else." It is possible, although it requires further research, that girls and women, charged with the maintenance of family ties, shoulder more of the "translation" responsibilities than male siblings and view their role as integral to the family's well-being, rather than an individual sacrifice. A Nicaraguan daughter-translator explains, "My mom came [to the U.S.] because she wanted a better life for us. She wants me to get a good education, and this is what I can do to repay her" (Stockwell: 2000).

The reason we came here, my mother had a lot of problems, money situations. But again, my family was always there for us, too. But she felt kind of embarrassed to ask for help ... I'd try to help her as much as possible, you know, like taking care of my little sister while she was working. She had two jobs. She was working during morning and nights to support us. And even though it was very hard, she wanted us to go to a private school. She always tried to give us the best, the excellent education for us.

—"Refusing the Betrayal: Latinas Redefining Gender, Sexuality, Family, and Home" (Fine & Weis: 1998)

Contrary to popular assumption, family responsibilities and unpaid labor may not negatively affect achievement. A study of high- and low-achieving Latinas in the San Diego City Schools finds that high achievers tend to have *more* responsibility at home than low achievers. Half of the high achievers take care of younger siblings in comparison with 20 percent of the low achievers. The majority of all Latinas—70 percent of the high achievers and 80 percent of the low achievers—also report paid work experience in addition to family responsibilities (San Diego City Schools: 1989).

On a more abstract level, children are aware of the limitations their families face and may curtail their educational goals to remain in line with their perceptions of their parents' ability to support them in their choices (Ginorio & Huston: 2000; Ginorio & Grignon: 2000).

Migration Patterns and Farm Work

While immigration status is a relatively common variable in studies, few studies explore the impact of migration. Children of migrant workers are more likely to transfer frequently and miss school—primarily to act as translators for their parents (Martínez, Scott, Cranston-Gingras, & Platt: 1994). According to the Migrant Attrition Project, the dropout rate for migrant students is close to half (Pérez: 2000). Yet migrant students are notoriously underidentified and underreported in states with large Hispanic populations. A recent preliminary study found that 70 percent of migrant students in districts with large Latino populations were not identified as they moved to a new campus (Pérez: 2000). A qualitative study of Latina migrant mothers who traveled with their families to pick tomatoes in northeastern Pennsylvania reveal contradictory values that they and their children experience, particularly around differences in sex roles between their own and the dominant culture and the choice between continuing education to seek careers outside farm work or taking advantage of the *immediate* availability of work and the opportunity to

---

Family and School

For Latino students—particularly girls—child care is a common burden that can compete with school. One of six children, Magdaly Marroquín, 16, shares regular responsibility for babysitting her 3-year-old brother John until their mother, Bibiana, returns from work. Two days a week, the Guatemala native leaves her last class early at her Wheaton, Maryland, high school to collect John from daycare. Sometimes, she misses basketball practice. On other days, the babysitting task falls to her 13-year-old sister.

"It's hard sometimes," says Marroquín, "because you want to do your homework and ... he wants to play. Sometimes you can't go out at all."

For a long time she used her childcare duties as an excuse for blowing off her homework. Her stock refrain to her mother's questions about homework was "I did it during lunch." No more. Marroquín, who wants to teach math, says she knows her future hinges on her school performance. Says the 10th-grader, "I wanted to do something better with my life. Everything before was socializing."

—Magdaly Marroquín (Morse: 2000)

make money. Although Latina mothers would like to help their children out of the migrant life, they face daunting exigencies (Bressler: 1996).

Children raised by parents who settle in one community will have at least that community on which to rely for consistency and adult supervision. Children raised by parents who follow the growing season of various crops all over the country may be less likely to find themselves integrated into larger social structures that facilitate educational attainment in school.

Themes and Questions for Further Research:
- Work, family responsibilities, and education: how are family responsibilities allocated? How do they influence schooling and achievement?

Family Acculturation

When individuals or groups with different cultures come into contact, social and psychological processes take place that lead to changes in the culture of one or both groups. In cultures of equal status, the changes are assumed to be of equal magnitude for both groups. In the case of the United States, it is assumed that immigrants will change their culture to resemble that of the Anglo majority. Acculturation refers to changes wherein one group acquires some of the characteristic values or behaviors of the other without giving up its own values or behaviors. Assimilation refers to the acquisition of new values or behaviors that replace original values or behaviors with the intent of becoming like the group being copied.

Researchers try to measure the acculturation of immigrant groups in a variety of ways, such as years or generations of residence in the United States, use of the English language, educational attainment, and number of non-Latina/o friends. Conversely, they may measure attachment to Latino culture by use of the Spanish language, participation in Latino cultural festivals, and constructed scales of Spanish pride, among other indicators. The result of all this variable creation is that acculturation may refer to very different things from one study to another. Unlike assimilation, which requires the abandonment of the culture of origin, acculturation does not necessarily involve the rejection of one culture for another. Families attached to Latino culture are not necessarily less attached to Anglo culture. It is entirely possible—and even beneficial—for Latinas to maintain strong ties to their Latino heritage while simultaneously participating in Anglo culture (Gómez & Fassinger: 1994; Valenzuela: 1999).

The ongoing, heated debate over who is to "blame" for the low academic achievement of many ethno-racial minorities has often centered on the culture of the ethnic group in question. Researcher Guadalupe Valdés explains: "In its strongest form, proponents of [the culture argument] argue that poor children are trapped in a culture of poverty and locked into a cycle of failure. Those who subscribe to this position maintain that children succeed in school only if their many deficiencies are corrected and if they are taught to behave in more traditionally mainstream ways" (Valdés: 1997, p. 398). Others have suggested that renouncing one's culture of origin actually deters achievement through a subtraction of cultural and linguistic resources critical to success (Valenzuela: 1999) and that the best path to economic well-being lies through celebrating one's culture while simultaneously participating in the institutions of the dominant culture.

For Latino families, much of the discussion around acculturation and academic achievement centers on language. In general, Latina/o parents seem to support their children's participation in Anglo culture through the use of the English language (LaVelle: 1996).

Lack of familiarity with the English language or lack of understanding of how schools work may have a negative effect on parents' ability to either help their children with schoolwork or effectively interact with school personnel on their children's behalf. Despite a nearly universal desire to help with homework, only 77 percent of Latina mothers surveyed felt they could help with reading and 66 percent with math (compared with 97 percent and 86 percent of Anglo mothers) (Stevenson, Chen, & Uttal: 1990). Hispanic parents with similar characteristics to other parents in all other aspects (evaluation of the child, definition of giftedness, etc.) are significantly less likely to request that a school test their child for placement in a gifted classroom (Scott, Perou, & Urbano: 1992). This tendency to be less likely to pursue enrollment in gifted programs could be due to language differences between parents and school personnel, or cultural views that hold excellence as something to be achieved and recognized in the group—not the individual.

In a qualitative study of tracking practices across several communities in Baltimore, first-generation Americans whose parents emigrated from countries "linguistically and culturally distinct from the U.S." described how the families' "social positions as immigrants also limited the families' understanding of the American educational system. As a result, these families heeded the advice of teachers and counselors who sometimes recommended that students move up the tracking hierarchy, but more often suggested that students move down" (Yonezawa: 1998, p. 9).

Children are sometimes caught between their families' efforts at cultural retention and their own exposure to the larger culture through media, peers, and schools. Some children end up feeling alienated from Anglo school culture, as well as from the culture of their parents. In these cases, children may adopt an urban street culture that has more in common with other urban youth than with other Spanish-speaking children or with Anglo classmates at school (Katz: 1996). Children who present themselves as part of the urban street culture are easy for teachers to stereotype and discount or dismiss, regardless of their actual participation in it, or their true academic abilities or aspirations (Valenzuela: 1999). This is one route through which a student's sense of self becomes bifurcated, leaving some students to disengage from education.

Values, Expectations, and Norms

Most Latina/o parents value education and encourage their children to do well in school (Huston, Ginorio, Frevert, & Bierman: 1996; Romo & Falbo: 1996). More than 90 percent of Latina/o children report that their parents want them to go to college—the same rate that Anglos report (Smith: 1995). Latina/o students in high school are as likely as Anglo students to report that their parents check their homework, talk about their classes and studies, limit their social and TV activities, and visit their classrooms (U.S. Department of Education: 1995).

Academic success is seen as the ticket to a better life for both the child and the entire family, especially in a context where the American Dream is a powerful incentive for immigration and heavily promoted in the schools and popular culture. However, this desire for academic achievement must be embedded within other cultural values. For example, Latino families commonly value respect for authority over individual assertiveness (Vásquez-Nuttall & Romero-García: 1989) and reward achievement most highly when it benefits the collective. The Latino emphasis on respect as part of education (Valenzuela: 1999) may lead to students being labeled apathetic or insolent and receiving less attention in the classroom than their Anglo peers. This value system runs contrary to the Anglo school culture, where individual achievement is prized over group achievement, where outspoken—even aggressive—students receive more attention in the competitive classroom, and where submissive behavior is seen as a negative trait, often associated with a lack of engagement (Vásquez-Nuttall & Romero-García: 1989).

Women are strong in spirit and I think they are stronger than men emotionally. It is better for them to make their minds strong. They are just going to be a strong person. They are the—how do you say it—the prop for the family. They are the head of the household—the kids and everything. The kids look up to them. They go to them for advice. They don't go to the father—well sometimes. The woman has to be strong.

—AAUW Educational Foundation, focus group with high school Latinas on education, Los Angeles, 1998

Parents may also hold expectations about children's commitments to the family (as exhibited through work, participation in religious activities, choices in residential location, etc.) that run contrary to the expectations of the school system. Furthermore, these expectations may be affected by gender norms within the culture, a possibility we discuss at more length in the next section.

Although education in the abstract is valued, many families are ambivalent about the American school system, having encountered and resisted the assimilationist approach prevalent in many schools (Brown & Stent: 1977). Families unfamiliar with and often alienated by school may have a generalized fear and distrust of the educational system (Rendón & Amaury: 1987), which leads to decreased involvement in educational programs. For example, Latino families are less likely than others to take advantage of preschool programs for their children, even after controlling for income, employment status, and education (Fuller, Eggers-Piérola, Holloway, Liang, & Rambaud: 1996). From 1973 to 1993, Hispanic three- and four-year-old preschool enrollments remained flat (at 15 percent), while White preschool enrollments steadily grew from 18 to 35 percent. White and African American preschool enrollments were roughly equal in 1995, yet

Schoolwork Comes First

Luisa Camacho, mother of 4-year-old Chantelle, 10-year-old Cheri, and 9-year-old Sharon, says she doesn't worry that her daughters may drop out of school one day. The girls—born here after Camacho emigrated from the Dominican Republic 10 years ago—know education is "muy importante," says their mother, that homework has precedence over "televisión." "They love to study," she says. "They can get whatever they need as long as they study. Education is a top priority."

After Sharon began attending weekend sessions of a support program called Educación 2000, the sprinkling of C's on her report card turned into A's and B's. The fourth-grader, who attends school in Prince George's County, Maryland, credits hard work and positive thinking: "Always listen to your teacher and do your work, and think good stuff," she says, "and don't think you're gonna get bad grades, because if you think that, you will."

—Luisa Camacho (Morse: 2000)

Hispanic enrollment continued to lag, despite considerable learning advantages associated with *quality* preschool programs (President's Advisory Commission: 1996; U.S. Department of Education: 1995). Parents with preschool children perceive a mismatch between the school's expectations for children and those endorsed by the family. The President's Advisory Commission on Educational Excellence for Hispanic Americans confirms this, noting that "low-income Hispanic families often believe their home environments are better for their children than programs like Head Start, because many early childhood services are not prepared to deal with the linguistic and cultural diversity of their children" (President's Advisory Commission: 1996, p. 2).

At the other end of the educational process, postsecondary education is often perceived as coming at the cost of maintaining close family ties and personal interdependencies that are highly valued in Latino culture (Ginorio & Martinez: 1998; Seymour & Hewitt: 1997). Schools that dismiss or simply overlook the importance of family support fail to capitalize on an important factor in the success of Latinas. Research by Helen García and another study by Norma Martínez-Rogers found that family support was mentioned repeatedly by Latina doctoral recipients, most of whom were first-generation women college students. The great majority named family and community involvement as measures of their personal worth and academic success (Why Hispanic-American: 1998). As in other cultures, women are charged with the maintenance of family ties. Thus, for many Latinas, possible selves imagined for the postsecondary years must include some integration of those conflicting expectations, or they will be forced to choose between education or loyalty to the family.

Gender Role Socialization

Given the centrality of the family in many Latino cultures, it is unsurprising that many families emphasize or highly esteem traditional roles for women as wives and mothers. Although there is variance within families and Latino cultures on this issue, residual, traditional expectations for women persist. For example, among Puerto Ricans with lower socioeconomic status (SES), gender roles for women are extremely restrictive; many traditional adults question the value of any education for women (Vásquez-Nuttall & Romero-García: 1989). For many Latinas, however, this traditionalism interacts with educational expectations and family ambitions to produce conflict for young women trying to follow contradictory prescriptions (González: 1988; Flores-Niemann, Romero, & Arbona: 2000).

The point is nobody really went to college and my parents—I'm the last girl at home—my parents are looking at me saying okay, you have to do this and you have to do that. They set my goals for me but it is my choice if I want to follow what they want me to do. To prove to them, to make them happy—I have to go by their rules.

—AAUW Educational Foundation, focus group with high school Latinas on education, Los Angeles, 1998

Conflicts about gender-appropriate behavior are another element that may bifurcate Latinas' sense of their possible selves. Parents see peer influence as affecting their daughters more than their sons and therefore closely monitor or restrict their daughters' activities as a guidance strategy (Azmitia & Brown: 1999). This strategy remains active even at the college level where parents prefer that unmarried daughters live at home (Guerra: 1996). Alternately, parents may see Latino-affirming schools as places where girls can explore and harmonize various gender roles and expectations.

PREGNANCY AND SEXUALITY

Teen pregnancy has often been treated as a health crisis in the United States—one that limits educational opportunities for both mother and child. Both families and schools play an important role in this phenomenon. Because the subject demands more attention, we have moved this discussion to its own section.

Family and Sociocultural Factors

The roles of mother and/or wife are highly valued for women in virtually all cultures. However, every culture has expectations about what constitutes acceptable timing of these events in the course of life. Teenage motherhood is considered a natural, normal process in many cultures. Many Latinas in this country come from areas where teenagers often marry and bear children as their primary (or only) rite of passage to adulthood, and the status associated with these events is highly rewarding. Researcher Pamela Erickson notes, "Pregnant women are afforded a prestigious position. ... For many young women from disadvantaged homes ... pregnancy may be the first time in a long time that they have received attention and respect." Ideally, the communities where this idea is prevalent are also organized so as to better support young couples with minimum education and life experience (Erickson: 1998).

> *Having a baby is a lottery ticket for many teenagers. It brings with it at least the dream of something better, and if the dream fails, not much is lost. If America cares about its young people, it must make them feel they have a rich array of choices, so that having a baby is not the only or the most attractive option on the horizon.*
>
> —Kristen Luker, 1997

In the United States, marriage and motherhood are more likely to be rewarded by middle-class Anglo society if they occur after high school and preferably after college. Pregnancy has particular relevance for Latinas. The National Center for Health Statistics reported in 1998 that for the first time, Hispanic teenagers are having babies at higher rates than White or African American girls. Almost 11 percent of Latinas aged 15-19 gave birth in 1995 (this figure describes births rather than pregnancy rates).

The effect of pregnancy on Latinas' educational achievement, however, is ambiguous. One comparative study found that teen birth was the most predictive factor of the chances of a Latina's dropping out of school. The only other significant predictor found in that study was whether or not the family received federal aid (Forste & Tienda: 1992). Latinas tend to cite concerns about sex and pregnancy at earlier ages than their Anglo and Asian age peers (Haag: 1999), although Latinas drop out due to pregnancy at about the same rate as Anglo girls. Three out of 10 Latinas report leaving school due to pregnancy, despite their higher rates of childbearing during the high school years (Forste & Tienda: 1992; Portner: 1998; U.S. Department of Education: 1995; Smith: 1995; Kaplan, 1990 cited by Erickson: 1998). Another study argues that the effect of teen marriage and pregnancy on high school completion was significant only for Whites, in both the short term (Forste & Tienda: 1992) and for eventual pursuit of postsecondary degrees (Rich & Kim: 1999).

It is not clear, then, that teen pregnancy precipitates a disruption of a low-SES Latina's life plan or trajectory (although it clashes with middle-class, Anglo culture and life plans), or that it would precipitate dropping out of school. In fact, a study of poor Latinas in East Los Angeles finds that the opposite may be true: although conventional wisdom holds that teen girls drop out of school because they are pregnant, a majority in this study (63 percent) were not attending school when they became pregnant. Dropping out of school may encourage Latina teen pregnancy, rather than the converse. We discuss this possibility below in the section on schools.

Once Latinas give birth, it is less likely that they will return to high school to complete a degree: only 27 percent of Latinas who gave birth during their teen years completed a degree by their mid-20s, compared to 55 percent among Whites and 67 percent of African Americans (Yawn, Yawn, & Brindis: 1997). Some research suggests that this may be so because teen Latinas, unlike African Americans, may not be encouraged to pursue further education once they are mothers, as they are "viewed as having entered the realm of motherhood with primary responsibilities for the home rather than finishing their education" (Yawn et al.: 1997). Indeed, although Latinas are more likely to be sexually active than Whites, they are also more likely to be married than other groups of girls (Yawn et al.: 1997).

As soon as I got out of high school I was pregnant but as soon as I had my baby I got right back in and this is like, what I'm going to do for the rest of my life and I'm not going to wait and not go to school because this is the money I'm going to be supporting my family with. So I've got to rush it.

—*AAUW Educational Foundation, focus group with high school Latinas on education, Los Angeles, 1998*

Family Support

Some studies suggest that strong family support is one major reason that higher birth rates among Latina teenagers do not lead to higher dropout rates (Romo & Falbo: 1996; Erickson: 1998). However, this support varies across Hispanic communities and according to immigration status. A 1995 study based on U.S. Census data shows that "foreign-born" young mothers, in a "distinctive immigrant strategy, especially for Mexicans," are more likely than their U.S.-born counterparts to rely on family resources and help to raise their children. Among young Latina mothers, economic support from families further differs, with Puerto Ricans appearing worse off financially than others, and Cuban mothers better off than other groups (Kahn & Berkowitz: 1995).

Schools

One of the most difficult subjects schools teach is sex education. Pressure from parents and community members often results in sexual education ending up on the "evaded" curriculum—never discussed, and its side effects ignored and relegated to the area of "personal problems." Even if sex education is taught as part of the formal curriculum in health class, *meaningful* school-based support systems for teen mothers are still relatively rare. Teen mothers rarely have good options for child care and alternative scheduling that will allow them to work toward, and complete, their high school degree. "Sex education school initiatives tend to place primary responsibility for adolescent pregnancy on girls" (AAUW Educational Foundation: 1998).

Furthermore, schools are implicated in this process when they are inattentive to students who are struggling: "Girls with previous academic difficulties (e.g., poor grades, grade retentions) were more likely to become pregnant, use drugs and alcohol, and engage in delinquent behavior" (AAUW Educational Foundation: 1998, p. 116).

Similarly, a 1998 sociological study argues that "girls who are discouraged at school will often escape through getting pregnant," which reverses the common argument that pregnancy precipitates dropping out. Manlove explains that among dropouts, female Hispanics have the highest rate of pregnancy at almost half (48 percent), and African Americans, the lowest at one-third (Manlove: 1998).

A study of the effects of pregnancy and childbearing on dropping out in the Southwest concludes that although pregnancy was one of the reasons (accounting for one-third of school dropouts), it was not the primary cause of dropping out among Latina females. Being behind a grade and traditional family sex roles emerged as important causes of dropping out (Kaplan:1990).

School then enters the equation on education in three distinct ways: conducting sex education classes to discourage pregnancy, offering support services to pregnant teens and young mothers, and ensuring that girls are engaged in school.

It's like I have to go to college because neither of my parents did. They know I do have high expectations for myself ... if I didn't go to college, my mom would kick me out. That is what I have to do. So it's like I have to prove to them that yes, I will do whatever I say I can.

—AAUW Educational Foundation, focus group with high school Latinas on education, Los Angeles, 1998

Among a sample of academically successful Latinas (mostly Puerto Rican), Thorne (1995) found low levels of sex role traditionalism. Adherence to traditional sex role stereotypes is a barrier to college retention (Castellanos & Fujitsubo: 1997; Flores-Niemann et al.: 2000). Research by Cardoza in 1991 found a strong relationship between sex-role status and college attendance and persistence among Hispanic women. Women who adhered to "traditional" sex roles (i.e., married with children or placing a high value on these qualities) were not attending or persisting in college to the same extent as "nontraditional" Latinas (Cardoza: 1991).

Themes and Questions for Further Research:
- How, if at all, do Latinas and Latinos differ in their views of education, and why?
- How does acculturation of women affect educational outcomes?

PEERS AND PEER GROUPS

While parental wishes and expectations clearly influence every student's life, peers can also play a pivotal role in either limiting or expanding a person's pool of possible selves. For girls still shaping their sense of self, peers play an important role in deterring or encouraging academic achievement and forming a self that aspires to academic excellence. The influence of peers can be either encouraging or dismissive of academically successful selves (Ginorio & Grignon: 2000; Ginorio & Huston: 2000). In a sample of rural girls, 40 percent report that their friends are supportive of their plans to go to college and 9 percent report that their friends are barriers to their college plans. Among a matched sample of dropouts and students who graduated, those who graduated were far more likely to have friends who did *not* drop out and who encouraged their success in high school. The author concludes, "The impact of peer group was a stronger determining factor in the student's decision to drop out or remain in school than any other factor with the exception of grades" (Valverde: 1987, p. 324). One area of discord between parents and children is the choice of friends whom parents often see as deterring their children, particularly boys, from "el buen camino" (the path of life) (Azmitia & Brown: 1999).

Adults often dictate different roles from those dictated by peers (Cohen, Blanc, Christman, Brown, & Sims: 1996, p. 60). Young people may be faced with pressure from their friends to choose among the stereotypical roles found within those communities. "Will they be 'schoolgirls' approved by adults, 'cool girls' popular with peers and doing well in school, or 'cholos' (sic) involved with gang culture?" (Cohen et al.: 1996). The strategy chosen by a particular girl will reflect not only her personal preferences but also the school setting. The choices for a Latina in a majority Latina/o school may be different from those she would make in a school where she is a distinct minority.

Peers', schools', and families' rewards and penalties for these roles and behaviors are not always in agreement. For example, both schools and families may be opposed to premature sexual activity even while boyfriends (and the larger peer network) encourage a young woman to engage in sex. Furthermore, while schools and parents are opposed to this activity, the sanctions each would impose on sexually active women may be quite different. Of particular importance is the 33 percent of 10th grade girls who report that boyfriends or fiancés make it more difficult for them to go to college (Ginorio & Grignon: 2000; Ginorio & Huston: 2000). This finding at the high school level is consistent with college-level findings that more traditional Latinas worry about being labeled too educated by prospective Latino husbands. Therefore, a young woman's choices of possible selves may be conditioned not only by the pressures she perceives from these various sources, but also by her understanding of the consequences her choices may carry for those people who are most important to her.

Some peers resent Latinas' engagement and success in school, and Latinas who do well in their classes may find themselves the target of harassment.

> *In DeAnza Montoya's Santa Fe Latina neighborhood, it was considered "Anglo" or "nerdy" to do well in school. So DeAnza cruised in wildly painted cars with her "low rider" rides and didn't worry about the future. She claims she was simply doing what was expected of her: "In school they make you feel like dumb Mexican," she says, adding that the slights only bring Hispanics closer together.*
>
> —(Headden: 1997)

Many girls of color (regardless of ethnicity/culture) report that they are accused of "acting White" when they try to engage in academic studies (Fordham: 1996; Dietrich: 1998; Haag: 1999). This perception of achievement as "White" is probably more pronounced in schools whose environment is perceived as assimilationist or dismissive of minority cultures. Often, this leads to a bifurcation of academic and Latina identity, making it difficult for a young woman to craft an identity that is both Latina and academically successful.

At the group level, participation in extracurricular activities (such as leadership, student government, and sports) has been reported as facilitating academic success. Among the factors that nurture academic ambivalence or rejection, gangs are the most discussed factor in the literature.

"Gangs" appear in the educational literature in two ways—as discouraging education by making schools less safe for particular individuals and as dismissing education by their oppositional relation to the adult authorities in school and society. Although popular media associates Latino gangs with males, around 3 percent of Latinas also participate in gangs (Rodríguez, personal communication: 2000). While few Latinas participate in gangs, their presence in the school environment and neighborhood may cause conflict or fear for personal safety among nongang members.

If gangs are present in the community, some Latinas will face pressure to participate in gang activities in their neighborhoods. Latina/os are almost three times as likely as Anglos to report having many gangs in their schools (Smith: 1995). The Department of Justice reports that in 1995, among students ages 12 to 19, half of Hispanic students reported that street gangs were present in their schools, an increase of 18 percent from 1989. Hispanics were two times more likely than all other groups of students to report gangs in their schools (Educational Testing Service: 1998). There is little research on how these experiences affect Latinas specifically.

Researchers believe that gang formation for boys or girls from any ethnic/racial group results from feelings of alienation from other institutions such as the family or school. Gangs thereby function as a support system and community (Katz: 1996).

> *They gave me power that I never had. At home, I was always the mother, always taking care of the kids. Getting no respect, never going anywhere because I was too young, this and that.*
>
> —Latina gang member quoted in "Women, Men, and Gangs" (Portillos: 1999)

Portillos notes that Latina gangs are hardly a sign of "liberation," but rather one strategy whereby Latinas deal with a bleak present and a harsh future that seems to offer little hope. A study of Hispanic girl gangs in New York describes that members "exist in an environment that has little to offer young women of color. The possibility of a decent career outside of 'domestic servant' is practically nonexistent. Most have dropped out of school and have no marketable skills. Future aspirations are both gendered and unrealistic" (Chesney-Lind & Hagedorn: 1999, p. 215). Gang membership usually involves ditching classes and a general disdain for the formal educational process. In Harris's 1988 study of gang members, none of the respondents had finished high school.

Risk Factors Related to Peer Culture and School

Recent research by the Urban Institute and the Commonwealth Fund explores teen risk-taking and risky behaviors such as using alcohol, tobacco, marijuana, or other illegal drugs; binge drinking; fighting; carrying weapons; thinking about or attempting suicide; and engaging in sexual activity. These reports found that Hispanic and White girls were more likely to engage in risky behaviors and take multiple risks than African American or Asian American girls (Commonwealth Fund: 1997). While teen involvement with these "risk behaviors" has declined overall over the past decade, this has not been the case for Hispanic males and females. The share of Hispanic students engaging in five or more risk behaviors increased from 13 percent in 1991 to 19 percent in 1997, an increase of nearly 50 percent. Among Hispanic 9th and 10th graders, participation in five or more risk behaviors nearly doubled in the same time frame, while the number remained relatively stable for White and African American students (Lindberg, Boggess, Porter, & Williams: 2000).

Data from the U.S. Centers for Disease Control and Prevention on illegal drug use similarly find that Latinas are more likely to use marijuana, inhalants, and cocaine than their African American or White peers. Lifetime use of powder cocaine by Latinas (12.5 percent) is nearly twice that of White girls (7.5 percent), and more than 12 times that of African American girls (1 percent) (CDC: 1998). These figures, based on a sample of high school students, do not reflect risk behaviors among Latinas who have dropped out of school and are thus conservative estimates of actual drug use among adolescent Latinas.

Themes and Questions for Further Research:
- What is the role of boyfriends' educational aspirations in shaping young Latinas' educational plans?
- What school practices foster school disengagement among Latinos or Latinas?
- Is gang participation a result of school disengagement, or does school disengagement result from gang membership?
- Are there differences in Latinas' and Latinos' involvement with risky behaviors? If so, why?

SCHOOLS

A school with adequate resources, including teachers, technology, and support staff, may succeed well with students whose values and experiences harmonize with those of the school. However, these same well-equipped schools may be far less successful if the school is dismissive of education that is consonant with students' cultural background. These incongruities are likely to occur when the school adheres to a monocultural view of education—a view that defines the school experience, environment, and norms narrowly, with one kind of student in mind. Education-dismissive schools may lack adequate economic resources to provide education to *any* student, have detrimental tracking practices, and fail to address life circumstances and needs of any students. Since only 6 percent of the national budget is allocated to K-12 education and additional resources are based on property taxes, poor students and students of color are far more likely to attend underfunded schools (Fairchild: 1989; U.S. Department of Education: 1996a; Oakes: 1990). These schools have low test scores and graduation rates, and students within them are faced with increasing detachment to school because of the extreme dissonance between their school, family, and social worlds. But well-supported schools may still be dismissive of the education of Latina/os if they see these students in stereotypically negative ways.

Education-encouraging schools successful with students of color also fit a profile: they provide a good education—not just good instruction. They acknowledge and respect possible selves that arise from cultural backgrounds, and work with families to support and guide a rich and congruent pool of possible selves.

Schools also have different degrees of *human resources* in the communities around them. In areas characterized by high congruence between the goals of the school and the goals of families, a large number of parents participate in school planning, fundraising, and the curriculum. However, where schools fail to reach out to parents and provide a welcoming, supportive environment for their values and ideas, children are more likely to experience the bifurcation of their school and community possible selves.

Gándara (1995) cites many studies suggesting that racially concentrated schools produce lower achievement than racially integrated schools, possibly related to funding and the quality of teachers. Among her sample of professional first-generation Latinas, most attended integrated schools and considered this important for their educational success in college. In addition, residential and school segregation have been argued to promote linguistic and class isolation that deter academic attainment (Arias: 1986).

Preparation of Teachers to Work with Latina/o Students

Substantial evidence suggests that an individual teacher can have a profoundly positive effect on a child's eventual adult achievements. However, *as a group,* many teachers are underprepared or unprepared to deal effectively with gender issues in the classroom. Furthermore, Anglo school teachers have been criticized for their lack of preparation and interest in learning about their students who come from ethno-racial backgrounds different from their own (Rendón & Amaury: 1987). Even Latina/o teachers may not feel adequately prepared or equipped to deal with "limited English proficiency" students or predominantly Hispanic classrooms. A 1990 survey of 438 Latina/o teachers, 77 percent of whom were women, found that only 41 percent felt that they were "well prepared to teach Latina/o students" and only 34 percent felt well prepared to teach limited-English-proficient students (Monsivais: 1990).

Teachers have little in the way of college or in-service preparation for working with these populations, and Latina/o teachers are few and far between. In 1994, 12 percent of students were Hispanic, but only 4 percent of teachers were Hispanic (Meek: 1998).

We continue to prepare teachers for non-existent students: middle-class students who speak English and have plenty of resources at home.

—María Robledo Montecel, Intercultural Development Research Association (Archer: 1996)

Teachers may have trouble moving beyond their own stereotypes of Latinas' educational possibilities (or probabilities, in their minds) and thus promote an education-dismissive environment. Many Latina/o students report that their teachers did not encourage them to consider college (Rodríguez: 1993). Evidence suggests that Anglo teachers have lower expectations for the academic performance of Hispanic students than do Hispanic teachers and that these expectations may be a crucial—and rectifiable—element of teacher education. However, teachers' expectations about academic performance are related to a student's chances of attending college. When evaluating students who are expected to attend college, Anglo and Hispanic teachers had similar academic expectations for their students. In this way, teachers may be education-encouraging for individual students while simultaneously endorsing an education-dismissive environment. However, Hispanic teachers' evaluations remained high for non-college-bound students, while Anglo teachers' expectations were lower (So: 1987b).

Well-intentioned and committed teachers may also be hampered by state-dictated curricula, the effects of standardized testing (Patthey-Chávez: 1993), and the questionable application of the "standards" movement. Teachers in urban Hispanic schools also suffer great stress—much of it caused by a lack of administrative support, a lack of resources, and disengaged students (Bruno: 1983).

By the same token, effective, skilled teachers with an understanding of their students can make a substantial difference, particularly for Latinas who value personal connections with teachers. Some of the characteristics associated with Latinas' high achievement in school, by conventional measures, often diverge from the way education is delivered in public schools. Several studies find, for example, that high-achieving Latinas in K-12 and postsecondary education emphasize the role of "personalism" in accounting for their success. As a report from the San Diego City school district on high- and low-achieving Latinas explains, "the traditional Mexican culture values personalism; that is, warmth, expressions of personal interest, and connectedness with others." This report finds that "the things both groups like and dislike about attending their school focused on relational/human interaction aspects" (San Diego City Schools: 1989, p. 59). The study found that "worst" school experiences focused on negative human interaction and that, conversely, Mexican American girls "respond more positively to positive reinforcement than do Anglo females" or males in general. High achievers focused on the personal qualities of teachers and counselors, such as helpfulness, caring, and personal regard (San Diego City Schools: 1989, pp. 5-6). Valenzuela's work in Houston re-affirms this finding, leading her to assert that care from teachers is a prerequisite for Mexican American students' engagement with education (Valenzuela: 1999).

Among a sample of 9th grade Latinas who excelled in science, virtually all of them reported encouragement by one or more teachers to continue their studies (O'Halloran: 1995). A national study suggests that Latina/os are as likely as Anglos to say their teachers are interested in their students, teaching in their school is good, and discipline is fair (Smith: 1995). Other high-achieving Latinas cite cultural traditions, such as story telling, caring for others, interacting, and communicating with style, as particular strengths that encouraged academic success (García & Associates: 1998). Students characterized as likely to finish high school are significantly more satisfied with their schools than students who are at high risk of not graduating from high school. These students' satisfaction does not make them insensitive to their teachers' treatment of others; in fact, they are likely to say that teachers' treatment of their at-risk peers is unfair and distracting (Reyes & Jason: 1993).

Themes and Questions for Further Research:
- Are there teaching techniques and styles that are especially effective with Latina/o students? If so, what are they?
- How can teachers and counselors build on the strengths of the family to foster high educational expectations among Latinas?

Counseling

Guidance counselors play a potentially powerful role—whether positive or negative—in students' lives and for Latinas, who may especially value personalized interaction with a school administrator. Although counselors may come into contact with children only once or twice a year, they greatly influence which courses a student will take and which tracks the child might pursue. They also formally supervise students' course-taking during secondary education and the preparation of students for academic opportunities beyond high school. In this regard, counselors are critical to young people envisioning their possible selves. However, their cursory contact with each student may necessarily limit their positive impact.

> *My counselor, I don't know. ... She tells you—you go in and tell her what you want to do and she'll tell you you can't do it. She picked out all your stuff and goes, no you can't do that. I told her I wanted to do something in medicine ... and she's like "nope, you can't. I'm sorry."*
>
> —AAUW Educational Foundation, focus group with Latina high school students on education, Los Angeles, 1998

The literature on counseling is quite mixed. Counselors have been accused of the same lack of preparation and interest as teachers, and some reports indicate that Latina/os are not so likely to use counselors as Anglo students, nor are counselors likely to reach out to Latina/os (Hispanic Children: 1985). Other reports indicate that Latina/os may have more contact with counselors than White students but related to nonacademic concerns such as discipline (Huston et al.: 1996). Counselors' low expectations of Latina/os' achievement lead them to place Latina/os in college preparation classes at much lower rates than their Anglo peers (Hispanic Children: 1985). In one study, half of the sampled Latinas who were excelling in their science classes in high school reported that their counselors were not at all helpful in their studies or career and college planning (O'Halloran: 1995). However, other reports indicate that Anglo and Hispanic sophomores in 1990 were equally likely to report that guidance counselors had encouraged them to go to college (U.S. Department of Education: 1995).

To the extent that counselors' interaction styles reflect or perpetuate Anglo cultural values, they contribute to the creation of an environment that may be overtly or covertly hostile to young people from cultures not versed in tracking, school bureaucracies, SAT tests, financial aid options, or the college admissions process. In one study of students' perceptions of counselors, Anglo-acculturated students were significantly more likely to rate a counselor as trustworthy than were bicultural or Latino-acculturated students. Furthermore, Latino-acculturated students seemed to prefer a different counseling style and were significantly more likely to rate a counselor using a nondirective style as being more understanding of their problems and needs (Pomales & Williams: 1989).

> *My college counselor at my high school ... wasn't supportive of me at all, because I did have low grades at the time, but I still thought I could do whatever I really wanted to and she just didn't recommend me to apply to any of my colleges. Even though I did, I got accepted to every single one. I made her feel real stupid.*
>
> —AAUW Educational Foundation, focus group with Latina high school students on education, Los Angeles, 1998

Case studies suggest that guidance counselors can help a young woman better manage demands placed on her time by providing flexible scheduling options, suggesting tutoring programs as appropriate, and recommending other academically supportive programs. In these cases, counselors can serve as significant ambassadors between the Latina student and the worlds of college, work, and after-school programs, even if that support is short-lived or limited in scope (Romo & Falbo: 1996).

English as a Second Language Classes

English as a Second Language (ESL) classes are too complex and contentious an issue to cover fully in this review, yet they must be mentioned as a critical component of Latinas' school experience. The U.S. Department of Education's Office for Civil Rights shows that nationally, a substantial percentage of Hispanic students—40 percent of males and 37 percent of females—are identified as "in need of LEP [Limited English Proficiency]" classes or programs, and the same percentages are in fact "enrolled in LEP" (Office for Civil Rights: 1999).

ESL classes provide education in basic academic subjects in Spanish, while offering intensive English language classes concurrently. A great deal of research and theory suggests that doing away with ESL classes would be a disservice to students: for many, these classes are essential for building strong basic skills. Some evidence indicates that students—at least those in integrated schools—find language-based tracking useful because it separates them from an otherwise hostile environment and cocoons them with teachers and peers who support their success and ambition (Gándara: 1995). Furthermore, to deny students a learning environment that supports their native language, some researchers conclude, "guarantee(s) ... intellectual passivity" (Fuentes: 1994) and may limit their cognitive proficiency, which is best developed through a language in which students are fluent.

However, in many districts, there are serious ramifications to being placed in the ESL track. Once in an ESL track (where classes are usually remedial and rarely college-preparatory), students have a very difficult time moving into mainstream classes even if they excel in school and have their parents' and teachers' support (Romo & Falbo: 1996). Students themselves say that language classes contribute to the stereotyping and maintenance of a social hierarchy in which they are forever on the bottom rung (Burke: 1995; Genesee & Gándara: 1999; Genesee: 1999). Some argue that this segregation deters academic attainment by narrowing a student's options—especially of entering college, but even for receiving a high school diploma (Arias: 1986).

Themes and Questions for Further Research:
- There is a need for further research on peer and gender relations in the context of ESL programs and classes that stereotype Latina/os.

School Climate

Few students negotiate the time from youth to adulthood without being taunted or faced with peer harassment at some point. Evidence suggests, however, that Latinas are more likely than Anglos to feel that their education is interrupted by other students, to feel unsafe, and to see fights between different racial/ethnic groups (Smith: 1995). Latinas are more likely to fear for their personal safety in school (7.7 percent) than White (2.5 percent) or African American girls (6.1 percent), and express more apprehension than their male peers (6.8 percent). Only African American boys expressed the same level of fear about going to school as Latinas (7.5 percent) (CDC: 1998).

According to 1996 national data from the Department of Education, Latina/os generally are the most likely to report feeling unsafe or very unsafe at school, more than African American or White students (13 percent to 9 percent and 8 percent, respectively). Other national data support this conclusion. Data in 1992 from a longitudinal study found that Hispanics were more likely than White students to agree that they "don't feel safe at this school" (15 percent to 9 percent) and to report that "fights often occur between different racial/ethnic groups" (32 percent to 21 percent) (Educational Testing Service: 1998).

Recent research on Hispanic education extends the idea of "safety" to the idea of "social or psychological safety" in the classroom and the learning process. Students feel psychologically safe and comfortable in classrooms, in one student's terms, "when all of my other classmates respect me and they don't mess around. When you don't have side comments, like sometimes when I try to speak in front of a class because I'm afraid of what people are going to say" (Shivley: 2000, p. 3).

Compounding this issue is gender. Latinas are at double jeopardy even before we consider all the other touchstones for childhood insult (social class, language, physical traits, etc.). Recent qualitative research finds that Latinas more often than girls of other racial/ethnic groups say that they have been the targets of sexual slurs and, significantly, insults against their intelligence (Haag: 1999). Previous research indicates differences along ethnic lines among young children, where 10 percent of Latinas report sexual harassment before the 3rd grade (AAUW Educational Foundation: 1993). Girls who report being the target of sexual harassment are likely to experience a range of negative outcomes, such as not wanting to go to school, not wanting to talk as much in class, and not being able to pay attention (AAUW Educational Foundation: 1993).

While many are loath to use the word, students do report experiencing racism in their schools. At its most subtle, they report negative stereotyping by teachers and peers (Burke: 1995), while others report overt statements about inherent capabilities (or the lack thereof). For example, a "frustrated White teacher told [students] that 'we had no futures' cause we were Hispanic, that we'd never get out of Avila, that we'd work at McDonald's" (Cohen et al.: 1996, p. 58). In other cases, teachers and counselors assume that students who speak Spanish are gang members (Romo & Falbo: 1996). Urciuoli argues that such behavior flows from the racializing of Spanish speakers, a process by which people who "use languages other than English in public and in ways that are not ... unequivocally middle class presentation ... are seen as dangerously out of order" (Urciuoli: 1996, p. 38).

A 1989 San Diego school system study of high- and low-achieving Latinas gathered qualitative evidence of racist comments and tendencies in the schools. "Mexican students tend not be included in activities here," one Latina writes. "Mexican girls aren't allowed to be cheerleaders and are not featured in the yearbook. Students ... think Mexicans have no ability. They walk away from us." Another reports that her "10th grade English teacher was very prejudiced. She ignored me and other Hispanics when we raised our hands. Lots of students and parents complained." These comments cut across achievement levels, as did experiences with peers. "Some White girls tease and call me Chola and mimic Mexican accents in the bathroom," one writes. When asked what they didn't like about school, low and high achievers alike pointed most often to unpleasant or hostile incidents with peers and teachers, often involving racial tensions or insults (e.g., "people making fun of your clothes," "some White kids feel superior to Mexicans and [B]lacks", "some people are prejudiced, not used to Hispanics") (San Diego City Schools: 1989, p. 6).

For nearly 10 months of the year, most children spend six to eight hours a day in school. For children of color, school is often an environment immediately associated with tension: to fit in and be accepted by the dominant institution, they are pushed to distance themselves from their culture of origin. First-generation students have to learn a new language (both verbal and nonverbal), abide by cultural norms that may diverge from those they practice at home, and negotiate a system that was probably designed with a very different generic student in mind. The prototypical student has at least some cultural capital: educated parents, fluency with English (and no accent), access to financial support for educational and cultural activities, familiarity with the educational "system," and few other responsibilities to detract from full-time attention to schooling and extracurricular activities. Children undoubtedly do their best to walk the line between acceptance in school and the maintenance of ties to their home culture. Yet many face a seemingly immovable system which neither they nor their parents are able to negotiate. By the time they reach high school they are set in adverse tracks of low-level or remedial classes that perpetuate boredom and mutual disinterest: the system doesn't care about them and, by then, many of them no longer care about the system (Valenzuela: 1999).

Transition to Work or College

Most educational research assumes that high school graduates will, or ideally should, enroll in college immediately following high school. However, a large number of students choose to work or enter the military upon high school completion. For some of these young adults, college will come—but later. Still, the direct high-school-to-college transition is the path that leads to the greatest likelihood that a student will complete a college degree within 10 years of high school graduation (Adelman: 1999).

> *Not every school does get [college] recruiters to come to a school. I think that would be a good thing because like something might interest them but they never really thought about it. If somebody would come and talk about it and not only talk about their occupations but college choices.*
>
> —AAUW Educational Foundation, focus group with Latina high school students on education, Los Angeles, 1998

Aside from the educational experiences and outcomes already discussed, the economic needs of their families and the type of *financial aid* packages available for their schools and programs of choice affect Latinas' college enrollment. At this transition point, Latinas' commitments to academic success may be tempered by their *preparedness to leave home*. To the extent that postsecondary schooling means leaving communities, families, and friends, choosing school may feel like a slight of their family's and friends' priorities. These two factors are especially significant at the moment of transition out of high school.

Financial Aid. Applications are notoriously difficult to read and understand—even for a parent for whom English is the first language. For Latina/o parents, these forms may deter application for scholarships and state aid—which in turn limits the number and types of schools a student considers for postsecondary education. Latina/os are more likely to attend less expensive community and state colleges, which offer fewer resources for financial aid. One study suggests that of the three-quarters of Latina/o parents eligible for aid, only half applied for it (So: 1984). Latina/o parents were severely undereducated about financial aid and less likely than Anglo parents to seek information about financial aid through formal channels (So: 1984). Furthermore, many forms of aid are applicable only to certain schools or specific fields of study (Rendón & Amaury: 1987; Mortenson: 2000). Therefore, students dependent on funding other than from their families for their college education may find their options severely constrained (So: 1984).

Leaving Home. Young adults differ in their eagerness and preparation to move away from home to attend school. For many, attachment to friends and family make this separation nearly impossible—a factor that may be particularly poignant for Latinas who come from a culture that emphasizes familial ties, particularly for women. Some women's families support their college aspirations only if they attend schools near home (Guerra: 1996; Wycoff: 1996). Latinas from small Latino towns or rural areas may also fear the prospect of moving into a larger, bewildering, if not intimidating, world for which many students have had little preparation (Ginorio & Huston: 2000; Ginorio & Grignon: 2000). These apprehensions may result in individuals choosing to attend college—such as community college—close to home. For those who do move away, the pull to return home may cause them to leave school before completing their degrees. Even when leaving for school means relocating 40 or 50 miles away, there may be some family resistance to girls going away to college (Ginorio & Huston: 2000; Ginorio & Grignon: 2000; Guerra 1996; Castro: 2000). This fascinating theme—which captures the dissonance between an individual Latina's educational goals and her other priorities and values in the family and community—certainly deserves further research and attention.

> *Why is higher education such a disappointing experience for us nowadays, particularly in private colleges? ... Is the American Dream accessible only when one denies one's own past? Once again, the young people are pushed to the margins, their journey from the barrio to the classroom marked by depression. ... When I was a graduate student at Columbia University from 1987 to 1990, not a single course was offered on Puerto Ricans on the mainland, although the school, on 116th St. and Broadway in New York, is surrounded by millions of Spanish-speaking Borinquens. ... While society is already accepting Latinos as a major economic and political force, private colleges hesitate.*
>
> —(Stavans: 1995)

Many middle-class students are prepared for college classrooms by received wisdom and informal knowledge acquired from friends, siblings, and parents who have been there and share their experiences. Many are able to attend camps and campus activities that familiarize them with college environments. Furthermore, many high school teachers—particularly those responsible for teaching college-prep classes—help students engage in anticipatory socialization. They help young people learn how to ask questions in the classroom, how to approach a teacher during office hours, or how to argue a grade. Latinas do not have the same access to this "cultural capital," and the conflicts of leaving home may weigh more heavily on young women than men, although the issue invites further research.

Themes and Questions for Further Research:
- How do concerns about leaving home at the high-school-to-college transition point influence Latinas' educational decisions?
- Most young adults who leave school before receiving a diploma are *not* gang members or teen parents. Yet little is known about minors who are not in school. How do their experiences differ from young people who may be just as disengaged from school, yet remain in the system? Is "getting out" truly the best option? What alternative schooling opportunities might benefit those who leave the public school system before graduation?

PART 3: INDIVIDUAL CHARACTERISTICS ASSOCIATED WITH EDUCATIONAL OUTCOMES

This section focuses on individual traits and variables that relate to educational processes. We have divided this section into two subsections, both linked to education: cultural factors (ethnic identification, language, and generational status) and self-efficacy factors (confidence, achievement motivation, and past performance).

CULTURE AND THE INDIVIDUAL

Educators and psychologists have studied the internalized aspects of society and culture and labeled them *identity*. Identity echoes the values of the families and communities where the individual grows up.

The development of a strong sense of identity is the central task of adolescence. Latina/os in the United States who are from families who are recent immigrants or who are retaining a commitment to the Latino culture face a double task. The task of learning two cultures is complicated by the different status of the two cultures. The experience of a Latina who grows up as a minority in a community is different from that of one who grows up in a Latino-majority community, even if both are equally aware of the often negative perception of Latina/os. These differences are magnified or extenuated by class and racial differences as well as Latino group (Mexican, Cuban, Puerto Rican, and so forth) and region.

Researchers measure acculturation in a variety of ways, often confounding several issues within one label or measurement tool. For example, coming from a home in which Spanish is the only language spoken is highly correlated with being the child of immigrants. Hence, researchers may utilize language spoken in the home as an indicator of generational status within the United States, and the resulting research cannot determine if the outcomes observed are due truly to language or actually to generational status or acculturation. Here we follow the trends in the literature and discuss linguistic ability and ethnic identity as separate issues, notwithstanding their interrelations.

Identity

The maintenance of a sense of ethnic identity in the face of overt and subtle discrimination can be a stressful, potentially exhausting process. Latina/os whose sense of self incorporates a Latino identity may be at odds with a school system that rewards only Anglo-identified traits and values. This tension can contribute to high absenteeism, lower engagement in the classroom, and higher dropout rates.

Latinas who are able to engage successfully in both Anglo and Latino culture are acculturated but not assimilated. Acculturated Latinas may be at a creative and cognitive advantage over those rooted in only one culture. The context determines whether biculturalism is stigmatizing or affirming. If biculturalism is perceived as a mark of low status, it can lead to stigmatization on the part of the majority. If it is perceived as an assimilationist move by other Latina/os, it can lead to stigmatization by that community (Urciuoli: 1996).

Gándara (1995) finds that Latina high achievers in her sample moved successfully and fluidly between the culture of the barrio or the fields and the culture of high-achieving Anglos, and were characterized by high adaptability. So (1987a, p. 30) finds evidence for the Hispanic reference group hypothesis: Students "who aspire to the middle class, as well as maintain strong communicative skills within the Hispanic culture, outperform [in GPA and standardized math and reading tests] those who do not aspire to the middle class and do not maintain strong communicative skills with their parents and reference group." Similarly, Gómez & Fassinger (1994) found that Latina undergraduates with a bicultural identity had a significantly broader repertoire of achieving styles than students who were classified as belonging to either the Anglo culture or the Hispanic culture.

Another way of capturing biculturalism is to assess an individual's comfort when submersed in a group dominated by Anglos. Steward, Germain, & Jackson (1992) found that among successful college students, interaction styles did not change with the ethnic/racial composition of the group. Lango (1995) also found that Latinas who had gone on to graduate school were significantly more comfortable in a group of Anglos than were senior Latinas at the same institution.

Linguistic Ability

One of the most important individual characteristics associated with educational achievement is a student's proficiency in English and/or Spanish. Language is often tied to an individual's socioeconomic status, migration history, and cultural commitment. The best studies control for these variables in an effort to isolate the actual effects of language, rather than confound those effects with socioeconomic status, migration, history, or culture.

The stereotype held by many individuals is that bilingualism is a detriment to student learning. It was long believed that children from Spanish-speaking homes needed to speak only English to succeed in American schools. Most studies that focus on language suggest that bilingual students are able to function more efficiently in both their home culture and the school culture—a point that argues that institutions may benefit students more when they support (rather than subtract from) family and community worlds (Viadero: 1996; Adams et al.: 1994). Students who are bilingual have larger information networks, leading to higher grades (Stanton-Salazar & Dornbusch: 1995) and higher graduation rates than those found among students who speak only English or Spanish, even after controlling for socioeconomic status (Rumberger & Larson: 1998).

False Assumptions

Halting English can be misread as lack of intelligence. "Everybody feels if you're a Spanish student, you're not very bright," complains 16-year-old Mercedes Aguilar. Mercedes, a vocal 10th-grader in Sandy Spring, Maryland, came to the United States from Guatemala two and a half years ago. "Teachers tell you things two, three times, like you don't understand. ... Okay, I get it," Aguilar finds herself thinking. "You don't have to repeat me two, three times."

Two of Mercedes' friends dropped out last year, one to have a baby. Mercedes says she won't join them. "I have a lot I want to do. For that I need high school." She has hopes of being a counselor. "What I want to do is help girls. ... They are the ones who most need help. Sometimes they don't find the right help, you know. They need help the most."

—Mercedes Aguilar (Morse: 2000)

Themes and Questions for Further Research:
- Does the incidence or effect of bilingualism or bilingual education differ for boys and girls? If so, how?
- How does bilingualism, or biculturalism, affect experiences with Anglo and Latina/o peers in schools and colleges?
- How does stigmatization of bilingualism/biculturalism affect Latinas' investment in education that is dismissive of Latina/o values?

SELF-EFFICACY

Students must have self-confidence or a sense of "efficacy" to implement the options they see for themselves in the future. Researchers identify the support and reactions of families, peers, teachers, and other important figures as central to this process of building confidence and efficacy. Latinas, on average, start school with higher self-esteem than their African American and Anglo peers (AAUW: 1991). A manifestation of this higher self-esteem may be seen in the anticipation that they would do very well in high school math and reading classes (Stevenson, Chen, & Uttal: 1990). However, decreases in self-esteem common to all girls as they progress to young adulthood are greater for Latinas than for other groups (AAUW: 1991). One probable source of this diminished self-confidence is the school environment itself. Although it requires further exploration, a recent qualitative study finds that Latinas wrote of being belittled intellectually more frequently than their African American and Anglo peers (Haag: 1999).

Self-confidence is negatively impacted by low grades because grades are used as an indicator of performance and potential. Receiving low grades may lead to early withdrawal from school (Valverde: 1987). However, intriguing anthropological data suggests that adult high-performing Latinas have not always done well in school and that even high-performing youngsters may withdraw emotionally and end up doing quite poorly in high school (Gándara: 1995).

In four-year colleges, as well, low grades among Latina/os are a strong indicator of the chances of dropping out (Rendón & Amaury: 1987). In addition, SAT scores are significantly predictive of first-year college grades, but not of retention in college among university Latina/os. A Latina's academic success (persistence through the degree) was correlated with a positive view of intellectual ability combined with a strong sense of responsibility for her academic future (Wycoff: 1996).

Compared with Anglos and American Indians, Hispanics have higher occupational aspirations (Farmer, Wardrop, & Rotella: 1999) but lower expectations for achieving them. Socioeconomic status affected self-efficacy among Hispanics. In terms of educational goals, a study of Latinas in Catholic school finds that they have slightly higher aspirations than their Anglo classmates (Lee: 1988), but national studies find lower educational goals than Anglos, perhaps reflecting the different opportunity structures offered to students in the public and private schooling systems (Smith: 1995).

As individuals face life, it is often assumed that at the moment of choice, the individual stands alone in making decisions about the present and about the future that he or she envisions. But qualitative research on high-achieving Latinas with doctoral degrees also notes the particular importance of mentoring and of supportive personal relationships. Gómez found in a qualitative study that all but one of her participants spoke of a pivotal individual who had a positive influence in their lives and career, and all had spouses or partners who supported and encouraged them. As we have argued throughout the previous sections, an individual's education is shaped by her or his family, school, and communities. Individual Latina experiences are contextualized by Latino values that are more communally oriented than those of the Anglo culture and by their position as an ethnic minority in the United States. Even for individuals for whom Latina identity is merely attributed, this ethnic attribution also affects their educational outcomes.

Themes and Questions for Further Research:
- What is the relationship of achievement, confidence, and persistence for Latinas?

PART 4: CONCLUSION AND RECOMMENDATIONS

Possible selves serve as bridges to the future. They are sustained or changed by the experiences of individuals in their daily lives and encouraged and limited by the people and resources accessible to them. Three large institutions consume most of the energy and time of most people in this society: family, education/work, and community. Thus these institutions shape the individual's possible selves.

This section explores two complementary issues: the ways individuals' possible selves operate regarding education and how families, education/work, and communities affect these possible selves. We will outline how the information presented in the previous three sections can be interpreted as affirming, encouraging, discouraging, and/or dismissive of educational possible selves.

Most young people's possible selves incorporate many important areas in their lives, such as family, school, peers, and community. The educational system assumes that the possible selves that students construct are internally consistent—that the selves will be building on each other. For example, schools assume that a student's family has the resources to have the student attend full-time, focus only on schoolwork, and move from high school directly to college after graduation. Schools may assume that the ethos of individual accomplishment and competition in the classroom harmonizes with the student's family or community ethos. They often assume that families envision as ideal a four-year college education that requires a daughter's or son's departure and a natural progression thereafter toward a professional career.

The discourse that posits educational possible selves assumes that education is the mandatory—and only—work of children. For most children under the age of 12 in the United States, play and education are indeed their only work. Among families where children have no other responsibility except that of studying and where their contributions to the family's well-being are defined in terms of doing well in school, the educational and familial possible selves blend and the educational possible self seems preeminent. Among Latinas, however, there are age and class differences regarding how much time and for how many years children can focus on their education. Poorer Latina/os have to attend to economic contributions to the family at an earlier age and for longer periods. Regardless of class, Latinas have greater cross-generational involvement and sense of responsibility to the family than do Anglos. This means a greater involvement of children in family activities, ranging from events such as parties and funerals to daily life. Among Latina/o poor families, even young girls often have other family responsibilities involving childcare and housework. As girls reach puberty, their family responsibilities increase. Thus, a Latina's possible selves as a family member are extensive and central to her identity and more differentiated from the educational possible selves than they are for Anglos, since schooling is not organized with these cultural characteristics and realities in mind.

Gender affects how closely the possible selves of student or worker and family member match. Latinas, who as high school students have already experienced incompatibilities between their educational and familial possible selves, may not envision themselves as college students. Precisely because the family is so important, Latinas may interrupt or leave their education earlier than other girls or women. Current and anticipated incompatibilities between their familial and work possible selves affect the career and curricular choices they make in college (Seymour & Hewitt: 1997).

EFFECTS OF FAMILY, SCHOOL, AND COMMUNITY ON EDUCATIONAL POSSIBLE SELVES

The congruence or incompatibility experienced by individuals among their possible selves is shaped by family, school, and community visions of what is possible for particular students as individuals and as members of socially defined groups such as Latinas. For young people, family, school, and peers are the main arenas for the affirmation, encouragement, discouragement, or dismissal of their educational possible selves. "Affirmation" and "encouragement" differ in that encouragement is support given to the individual student, while affirmation is support given to the value of education for a person as a member of a group. When support is denied, a similar distinction exists between dismissal and discouragement with discouragement being given to the student as an individual and dismissal to the student as a member of a group. Thus, one can find a teacher or school giving support to a Latina because she is exceptional (therefore perceived as different from other Latina/os) while the same teacher or school can dismiss the usefulness of education for most Latina/os as a group.

Whether through interviews (Gándara: 1995; Ginorio & Huston: 2000; Ginorio & Grignon: 2000) or surveys (Ginorio & Huston: 2000; Ginorio & Grignon: 2000; Rodríguez: 1993), Latina/os state that their families are their main source of support for pursuing their educational goals. More than 95 percent of families provide education-affirming support to students pursuing high school degrees. The level of education of the family determines whether the emotional support is accompanied by social and economic capital (Ginorio & Martínez: 1998).

There is another way in which families, the very people who may provide education-affirming information and support, may, by their very support, make it more difficult for the student to leave home when the time comes to go to college. Because familial possible selves are so central in a Latina's life, many Latinas report extreme levels of homesickness that prompt them to leave their college education if it cannot be resumed at a college near their home town (Ginorio & Marshall: in progress).

But families are also sources of discouragement for college-level educational pursuits. This discouragement is mostly due to the parents' opposition to the children, in particular their daughters, moving away from the family to pursue higher education (Guerra: 1996). There is also parental discouragement if the family does not have the resources to pay for the student's expenses while in college.

A lot of us don't have the money [for college]. I'm not going to depend on my parents to pay for my college. If they are going to help me, that is fine, but I want to say, "Yeah, I did it myself and I didn't need my parents." So I want to work. I want to save so that I can at least get a head start. I'm not going to just jump into something that I'm not prepared for.

I know it is going to be really hard because it is going to be really expensive. I have to go through a lot more education. That is what worries me about the future. How am I going to pay for all of that?

—AAUW Educational Foundation, focus group with high school Latinas on education, Los Angeles, 1998

A significant number of Latino families also have values and expectations that are education-discouraging in direct or indirect ways. Gendered values that place more responsibility for housework on girls and women have been documented as interfering with postsecondary education (Chacón et. al.: 1982). Women are also expected to do more of the emotional work regarding nurturance and connections in a family. Some families also have education-dismissive attitudes, especially for a daughter's need for education if she is presumed to become "only" a wife and mother (Vásquez-Nuttall & Romero-Garcia: 1989).

Many Latinas are faced with very real concerns that their educational goals are in conflict with expectations of their communities as well. For example, the relocation of a young woman who attends college away from home is often feared to be a permanent abandonment of the community. Furthermore, Latinas may believe that men of their ethnic background will not be interested in marrying a highly educated woman. Therefore, if a woman is interested in marriage, her options become marrying outside her community or reducing her educational aspirations to ones more in keeping with the desires of the men she'd most like to marry (González: 1988).

Communities are also significant sources of support for many students of color. Latinas often perceive their communities to be supportive of their high school education but not fully approving of Latinas who pursue higher education (González: 1988; Flores-Niemann et. al.: 2000), seeing them as aspiring to leave the community or making themselves different from community members.

Research on social experiences in college points to the importance for incoming students to find social worlds and communities that complement their academic activities. Mexican American students entering a large university "talk about the need to attach themselves to relevant social groups as a way to cope with the difficulties of 'getting in' to college." Tinto suggests that social membership supersedes academic membership for younger students who have left home to attend college (Tinto: 1997, p. 618). Another study of Mexican American students awarded the Ford Foundation Minority Fellowship identifies a positive mentoring experience as the "single most important" factor in obtaining a doctoral degree (Solorzano: 1992).

All schools are supposed to be education-affirming. Education-affirming schools for Latina/os in the United States would not dismiss the culture and history of the students and would focus on ethics and relationships (expressive orientation) (Valenzuela: 1999). While *educación* (in the Latino sense) encompasses the whole individual, in the United States education focuses on things and ideas (technical or instrumental orientation). Education-affirming schools would also challenge the students intellectually: the story of educator Jaime Escalante, featured in the movie *Stand and Deliver*, should be commonplace.

Teachers and counselors affect students profoundly, whether they encourage or discourage students' efforts. Many teachers, counselors, and staff encourage particular students whom they see as exceptional or with whom they have managed to establish personal relations. Students affirm the importance of this encouragement, identifying teachers and counselors as second only to parents in influencing their college ambitions (Ginorio & Huston: 2000; Ginorio & Grignon: 2000). In a moment of frustration a teacher may say, "You'll never leave Avila," and the statement becomes engraved in students' minds. For students who have strong educational possible selves and familial support, such a statement becomes a challenge to prove the teachers wrong, or it can be more easily dismissed as negative and unfair. For many other students with conflicted possible selves, such a statement is just another confirmation of the negative expectations the world has of them and another push toward academic disidentification.[8]

Education-dismissive schools may sound like an oxymoron, but literature suggests that many schools serving Latina/os do not affirm their education or build on the strengths and realities of these communities to help students mesh their educational, familial, and personal identities (Matute-Bianchi: 1986; Patthey-Chávez: 1993; Orenstein: 1994; Cohen et al.: 1996; Valenzuela: 1999).

In schools dismissive of the educational possible selves of Latina/os, even college-bound students may be discouraged (Patthey-Chávez: 1993). Under such conditions, large numbers of students are pushed out of schools. If they stay in school, Latinas may respond to dismissive education with silence. Alternatively, Latinas may get pregnant or engage in risky behaviors that manifest their alienation from schooling. Such behavior is often construed as an indication of a lack of interest and investment in education on the part of Latina/os. However, Valenzuela (1999) notes that students in Seguín High did "not oppose education," nor are they hostile to the idea of education as a road to social mobility. What they oppose is dismissive schooling—schooling where teachers see parents as liabilities and Latino values as deterrents to bright students' academic abilities. The existence of majority-Latino educational institutions does not guarantee the elimination of a dismissive education, if the values that *guide* the school do not respect Latina/os (Valenzuela: 1999).

At the institutional level, education-affirming schools would educate for "competence in the social world, wherein one respects the dignity and individuality of others" (Valenzuela: 1999, p. 23). When that occurs, students would not experience schools as a place for the bifurcation of their educational selves from their familial and community selves. The elimination of the resulting tensions would lead to higher levels of educational attainment for Latina/o students. For Latinas, high school and college can be places where they experience a bifurcation of their worlds and their possible selves. These possible selves build a bridge between the current state and the desired outcome (Oyserman & Markus: 1990 as cited in Cross & Markus: 1994). At the individual level they need a person who knows what it takes to get from here to there (Levine & Nidiffer: 1996).

> *About 3.4 million students entered kindergarten in U.S. public schools last fall, and already, at the dawn of their educational careers, researchers foresee widely different futures for them. Whether they are White, [B]lack, Hispanic, Native American, or Asian-American will, to a large extent, predict their success in school.*
>
> —(Johnston & Viadero: 2000)

Cross-school and cross-state data suggest that low graduation rates for Latina/os are not inevitable. Parenting experts have identified five factors that contribute to children's resiliency to complications like the temptation to leave school without a diploma: caring and support, high expectations, support to achieve those expectations, youth participation, and cross-generational relational involvement. Latinas possess many strengths and resiliencies that challenge the statistical portrait of what may be expected of them. Two findings that contradict the prevailing notions illustrate resiliency. First, although Latina teens have more babies than any other ethnic group, they do not drop out at any higher rate due to pregnancy. Second, retention and celebration of Latino culture and language actually seem to bolster their academic achievement (when combined with mastering the English language), rather than detract from it. We believe that both of these "non-intuitive" findings are attributable to strengths in the Latino community and family. Young mothers receive caring, support, and cross-generational involvement at very high rates within Latino communities, and successful biculturalism can occur only with intergenerational contact and participation, along with high expectations and support to achieve them. Schools, educators, counselors, parents, and other adults need to cultivate these resiliencies and cultural skills in their efforts to boost Latina/o educational achievement.

Graduation rates in high school and college are the result of social factors—factors for which we are all responsible. Even while individual teachers or counselors may be highly encouraging of individual Latinas, schools must take on the goal of developing climates in which education for *all* students is affirmed. These climates are marked by the assumption that all students have the capacity and desire to be academically challenged and to achieve academic excellence. It must be assumed—from the earliest possible moment—that the child needs to be prepared for lifelong education. This assumption must be embedded in teachers, counselors, parents, and, to the extent it is possible, peers. It must permeate everything from college-preparation tracks to ESL classes, including how children are drafted into these programs as well as the content of those programs.

RECOMMENDATIONS

The possible selves of all students are enhanced by enriched curricula, the proper training of school personnel, and high-quality communication between schools and parents. Toward that end, every child in the United States will benefit from the implementation of the following recommendations for school personnel, parents, and others:

- Help Latinas set firm, clear, realistic educational goals early on and scrutinize guidance counseling and advising to make sure those goals remain possible throughout the educational process. Academic counseling must begin in middle school and continue through high school to ensure that Latinas are not underrepresented in college-preparatory classes and they have full access to AP courses. Furthermore, advisors must curtail their tendencies to promote gender- and racially stereotyped careers; even from a very early age, children pick up on subtle clues as to the acceptability of their dreams and desires. Latinas need to hear from *all* the adults in their lives that college and professional careers are rewarding options and ones that they can achieve.

- Help students familiarize themselves with college environments, terminology, and prerequisites. Many Latinas come from families with little or no "cultural capital" to support their interest in college. College needs to be demystified—both for the young woman and her family—so as to promote her understanding that she has a place on the college campus. It is crucial that *families* are a part of this learning; they will better help their children aspire to college if they, themselves, are not daunted by it.

- Institute programs in schools that deal meaningfully with teen parenthood. This includes offering child care and alternative scheduling and promoting an environment in which a young mother is not labeled and treated as someone who is incapable of completing an academically rigorous program.

- Ensure that schools practice aggressive recruitment *out* of remedial tracks and supplement language-based tracking with challenging coursework and a positive attitude toward the future. ESL classes should not be used as holding tanks until the child is so frustrated and bored that he or she becomes disengaged from school.

- Encourage teaching programs to actively seek out a diverse student body, thereby providing future generations with teachers who more closely match the demographics of the school system. *All* teachers must be educated in techniques that are effective in working with students and families of color. This approach also should be instituted at colleges and universities within their own faculty and graduate schools.

- Discover and encourage financial aid opportunities that do *not* limit students' options for college and major. For students who rely on financial aid, current programs tend to track young adults into community colleges and part-time study—both of which carry less immediate financial cost. However, these options are also correlated with noncompletion of the desired college degree. Financial aid institutions need to take into account lost wages, commuting and housing costs, etc. Furthermore, these programs need to look at the economic needs of *high school* students as well as college students, and be prepared to extend financial aid to students who would otherwise be forced to leave high school to contribute to their family's income.

- Encourage research that accounts adequately for gender, race/ethnicity, and class in its construction of variables, analysis, and measurement. Researchers need to be consistent and clear in reporting their sampling techniques and careful when generalizing to larger populations.

For schools to be successful in assimilating language-minority students, they must do more than simply teach students English. They must also attend to and strengthen cultural awareness and identity so that language-minority students become bicultural as well as bilingual. ... [S]chools must not focus only on the academic curriculum; they must also work ardently on improving the social support system to engage students socially and reduce problem behaviors.

—*(Rumberger & Larson: 1998)*

address differences as well as similarities and implement programs designed to enhance the educational experience of students from backgrounds different from those of White middle-class males. Engaging all students in the educational process will decrease dropout rates, teen pregnancy rates, and gang involvement. It may also promote college enrollment and retention. To the extent that these are goals we all share, it is essential to discover and implement strategies for developing education-affirming environments for all students.

To achieve this, "school reform must be connected to girls' and boys' adolescent experience and developmental needs—both distinctive and shared" (Cohen et al.: 1996, p. 88). Furthermore, reform must be culturally relevant. Attempts to treat boys and girls as "the same" or to treat Latinas and Anglos as "the same" will only frustrate children in the group traditionally underserved by the school. Reform must

APPENDIX A: Methodology

Throughout this report, we have tried to be very specific about the populations discussed in terms of national origin, age, gender, social class, and so forth. However, much of the data published are not broken down below the level represented by the broad-reaching term "Hispanics," which the United States government uses in its reports. This catch-all label is useful when referring to population-wide trends, but it does not account for the differences among the diverse groups of people who are given that label. Each group brings its own history and culture to the United States and, in some cases, each group is as different from one another as they are from Anglos or African Americans or any other ethno-racial group.

The literature on Latina/os is also incomplete because it often fails to take into account how gender shapes these groups' experiences (Ginorio & Martínez: 1998). To the limited extent that Latina/os are the focus of educational research, these studies only occasionally integrate gender issues into their work and tend to do so by noting differences or similarities between boys and girls. While our aim was to include in this review only work that focused on Latinas, in many areas we had no choice but to include materials that did not account for gender in their analyses. The bulk of the articles covered in our discussion of trends in Latina/o educational performance are incomplete in this manner. We specify when we are reviewing research about the population as a whole and when we are drawing on studies that focus on or at least account for gender in their analyses.

By and large, we found very few articles that accounted for within-group differences such as social class, religious and political affiliations, specifics of ethnicity and ethnic identification, and documentation status. For example, the possible self an affluent Latina envisions may be very different from one envisioned by a poor Latina—a difference attributable to class and its attendant social/economic resources. Most sources also fail to account for the historical circumstances of a group's presence in the United States. For example, they may treat a political refugee—with all the rights that status confers in the United States—as essentially similar to a poor farmer from Central America seeking crop work in California or a recent Mexican immigrant as similar to a Mexican whose family has lived in the Southwest before the United States took over that land during the war with Mexico.

Furthermore, many countries contributing to the Latino population in the United States are characterized by large variations in ethnic identity, class, language, political affiliation, etc. Even in that minority of research that treats groups from different countries as potentially different, most researchers persist in treating populations from a single country as a homogeneous group. We urge readers to draw their conclusions after careful attention to the group label and level of specificity of the research.

The discussion section of this report draws on both qualitative and quantitative research relevant to Latinas and education. Some of the studies mentioned in the discussion section draw on national data, while others are based on samples of students. The latter are valuable, however, in pointing to avenues for further research and in providing rich case studies that illuminate the realities behind the national trends.

APPENDIX B: Summary of Data on Latinas for Selected States

Arizona

Latina/o Educational Attainment	Latinas		Latinos	
	Number	as percentage of total class population	Number	as percentage of total class population
Total Elementary and Secondary School Population	111,418	14	117,028	15
Latina/os diagnosed with or enrolled in				
Serious Emotional Disturbance (SED)	140	4	382	11
Specific Learning Disability (SLD)	3,988	10	8,343	22
Gifted and Talented (GATE)	2,347	5	2,528	6
AP Mathematics class	162	4	158	4
AP Science class	216	6	216	6
AP Computer Science class	6	2	19	6
	Number	as percentage of total population	Number	as percentage of total population
18-24 year olds enrolled in college	21,412	24	18,214	21
Latina/os 25 years and older with				
Less than 5th grade education	17,815	10.7	18,691	11.4
5th to 8th grade education	33,227	19.9	29,098	17.8
9th to 12th grade education (no diploma)	30,804	18.5	29,440	18.0
High school graduate	39,756	23.8	37,403	22.9
Some college	27,292	16.4	27,278	16.7
Associate degree	7,428	4.4	8,380	5.0
Bachelor's degree	7,172	4.3	8,153	4.8
Master's degree	2,018	1.2	2,720	1.6
Professional school degree	696	0.4	1,422	0.9
Doctoral degree	196	0.1	466	0.3

Sources: Office for Civil Rights (1999); U.S. Census Bureau (1993a)

California

Latina/o Educational Attainment	Latinas		Latinos	
	Number	as percentage of total class population	Number	as percentage of total class population
Total Elementary and Secondary School Population	1,142,140	20	1,186,660	20
Latina/os diagnosed with or enrolled in				
Serious Emotional Disturbance (SED)	416	4	1,360	13
Specific Learning Disability (SLD)	40,688	14	81,944	28
Gifted and Talented (GATE)	37,125	11	33,937	10
AP Mathematics class	3,605	8	3,515	8
AP Science class	2,446	7	2,392	6
AP Computer Science class	427	6	484	7
	Number	as percentage of total population	Number	as percentage of total population
18-24 year olds enrolled in college	270,434	23	204,559	18
Latina/os 25 years and older with				
Less than 5th grade education	290,118	16.0	305,750	16.1
5th to 8th grade education	342,847	18.8	348,864	18.4
9th to 12th grade education (no diploma)	366,154	20.1	385,531	20.4
High school graduate	358,609	19.7	336,516	17.8
Some college	248,801	13.6	267,252	14.1
Associate degree	96,195	5.2	95,424	5.0
Bachelor's degree	78,540	4.3	96,285	5.0
Master's degree	21,038	1.1	28,679	1.5
Professional school degree	11,068	0.6	18,932	1.0
Doctoral degree	2,732	0.2	5,777	0.3

Sources: Office for Civil Rights (1999); U.S. Census Bureau (1993a)

Colorado				
Latina/o Educational Attainment	Latinas		Latinos	
	Number	as percentage of total class population	Number	as percentage of total class population
Total Elementary and Secondary School Population	61,039	9	63,882	10
Latina/os diagnosed with or enrolled in				
Serious Emotional Disturbance (SED)	199	3	743	12
Specific Learning Disability (SLD)	2,198	7	4,228	14
Gifted and Talented (GATE)	2,599	6	2,652	7
AP Mathematics class	338	5	363	5
AP Science class	465	6	455	6
AP Computer Science class	36	4	59	6
	Number	as percentage of total population	Number	as percentage of total population
18-24 year olds enrolled in college	10,635	21	10,585	21
Latina/os 25 years and older with				
Less than 5th grade education	6,428	5.8	8,067	7.4
5th to 8th grade education	14,580	13.2	14,846	13.7
9th to 12th grade education (no diploma)	25,687	23.2	21,224	19.7
High school graduate	31,853	28.8	28,446	26.4
Some college	18,675	16.9	18,701	17.3
Associate degree	5,062	4.5	5,701	5.2
Bachelor's degree	5,641	5.1	6,938	6.4
Master's degree	1,757	1.5	2,473	2.2
Professional school degree	412	0.4	755	0.7
Doctoral degree	185	0.2	489	0.5

Sources: Office for Civil Rights (1999); U.S. Census Bureau (1993a)

Florida				
Latina/o Educational Attainment	Latinas		Latinos	
	Number	as percentage of total class population	Number	as percentage of total class population
Total Elementary and Secondary School Population	172,087	8	184,448	9
Latina/os diagnosed with or enrolled in				
Serious Emotional Disturbance (SED)	470	1	2,545	7
Specific Learning Disability (SLD)	6,122	4	14,432	11
Gifted and Talented (GATE)	6,071	7	6,141	7
AP Mathematics class	383	6	384	6
AP Science class	416	6	443	6
AP Computer Science class	8	1	36	6
	Number	as percentage of total population	Number	as percentage of total population
18-24 year olds enrolled in college	58,764	34	47,596	28
Latina/os 25 years and older with				
Less than 5th grade education	46,005	8.8	40,401	8.5
5th to 8th grade education	86,352	16.5	73,418	15.4
9th to 12th grade education (no diploma)	92,699	17.7	87,456	18.4
High school graduate	119,067	22.8	92,900	19.5
Some college	74,651	14.2	73,449	15.4
Associate degree	37,922	7.2	30,108	6.3
Bachelor's degree	43,068	8.2	44,295	9.3
Master's degree	11,822	2.2	13,108	2.7
Professional school degree	7,621	1.4	15,409	3.2
Doctoral degree	2,915	1.0	3,659	0.8

Sources: Office for Civil Rights (1999); U.S. Census Bureau (1993a)

New Mexico

Latina/o Educational Attainment	Latinas		Latinos	
	Number	as percentage of total class population	Number	as percentage of total class population
Total Elementary and Secondary School Population	77,792	24	81,644	25
Latina/os diagnosed with or enrolled in				
Serious Emotional Disturbance (SED)	248	8	1,104	36
Specific Learning Disability (SLD)	4,411	18	8,678	35
Gifted and Talented (GATE)	1,282	12	1,286	12
AP Mathematics class	480	14	513	15
AP Science class	211	16	317	24
AP Computer Science class	172	25	244	36

	Number	as percentage of total population	Number	as percentage of total population
18-24 year olds enrolled in college	16,988	27	14,724	23
Latina/os 25 years and older with				
Less than 5th grade education	12,174	7.5	12,498	8.3
5th to 8th grade education	22,803	14.2	19,751	13.1
9th to 12th grade education (no diploma)	30,654	19.1	27,303	18.2
High school graduate	52,795	32.9	46,232	30.8
Some college	24,472	15.2	23,652	15.7
Associate degree	5,596	3.4	5,285	3.5
Bachelor's degree	7,766	4.8	9,096	6.0
Master's degree	3,426	2.1	4,229	2.8
Professional school degree	615	0.4	1,157	0.7
Doctoral degree	124	0.1	596	0.3

Sources: Office for Civil Rights (1999); U.S. Census Bureau (1993a)

New York

Latina/o Educational Attainment	Latinas		Latinos	
	Number	as percentage of total class population	Number	as percentage of total class population
Total Elementary and Secondary School Population	243,272	9	256,945	9
Latina/os diagnosed with or enrolled in				
Serious Emotional Disturbance (SED)	1,376	4	6,022	17
Specific Learning Disability (SLD)	15,573	8	26,484	13
Gifted and Talented (GATE)	1,782	2	1,501	2
AP Mathematics class	94	1	102	1
AP Science class	124	1	127	1
AP Computer Science class	3	0.4	20	2

	Number	as percentage of total population	Number	as percentage of total population
18-24 year olds enrolled in college	82,763	30	64,890	24
Latina/os 25 years and older with				
Less than 5th grade education	73,798	11.2	52,113	9.2
5th to 8th grade education	105,851	16.1	82,206	14.6
9th to 12th grade education (no diploma)	150,440	22.9	138,869	24.7
High school graduate	154,296	23.5	131,256	23.4
Some college	83,252	12.6	78,344	13.9
Associate degree	31,388	4.7	21,960	3.9
Bachelor's degree	35,409	5.3	32,787	5.8
Master's degree	14,295	2.1	12,083	2.1
Professional school degree	5,664	0.9	8,755	1.5
Doctoral degree	1,579	0.2	2,310	0.4

Sources: Office for Civil Rights (1999); U.S. Census Bureau (1993a)

Texas				
Latina/o Educational Attainment	Latinas		Latinos	
	Number	as percentage of total class population	Number	as percentage of total class population
Total Elementary and Secondary School Population	695,185	18	733,850	19
Latina/os diagnosed with or enrolled in				
Serious Emotional Disturbance (SED)	2,366	6	7,241	20
Specific Learning Disability (SLD)	31,441	12	66,048	25
Gifted and Talented (GATE)	46,815	14	40,165	12
AP Mathematics class	3,732	11	3,702	11
AP Science class	4,068	11	3,448	9
AP Computer Science class	1,000	10	1,052	11
	Number	as percentage of total population	Number	as percentage of total population
18-24 year olds enrolled in college	133,859	24	113,224	20
Latina/os 25 years and older with				
Less than 5th grade education	207,113	19.0	190,362	18.2
5th to 8th grade education	213,432	19.6	195,723	18.7
9th to 12th grade education (no diploma)	182,994	16.8	190,160	18.2
High school graduate	232,331	21.4	205,058	19.6
Some college	138,822	12.7	138,949	13.3
Associate degree	36,784	3.3	40,689	3.9
Bachelor's degree	51,924	4.7	54,634	5.2
Master's degree	15,315	1.4	15,131	1.4
Professional school degree	4,731	0.4	9,944	0.9
Doctoral degree	1,108	0.1	2,527	0.2

Sources: Office for Civil Rights (1999); U.S. Census Bureau (1993a)

Arizona						
Labor Force Characteristics	State Population Total		Inside Metro Area		Outside Metro Area	
	Number	%	Number	%	Number	%
Employed Latinas over 16	107,572	15.0	89,270	83.0	18,302	17.0
Occupations						
Managerial & professional	17,420	16.2	14,586	16.3	2,834	15.5
Technical, sales, & admin. support	45,530	42.3	37,292	41.8	8,238	45.0
Service	27,069	25.2	21,914	24.5	5,155	28.2
Farming, forestry, & fishing	1,489	1.4	1,243	1.4	246	1.3
Precision, production, craft, & repair	3,859	3.6	3,480	3.9	379	2.1
Operators, fabricators, & laborers	12,205	11.3	10,755	12.0	1,450	7.9
Employment Sectors						
Agricultural	1,754	1.6				
Forestry & fisheries	75	0.1				
Mining	242	0.2				
Construction	959	0.9				
Manufacturing	13,981	13.0				
Transportation	4,629	4.3				
Wholesale	2,788	2.6				
Retail	22,716	21.1				
Finance	7,566	7.0				
Services	46,625	43.3				
Public Administration	6,237	5.8				

Source: U.S. Census Bureau: *1990 Census* (1993a)

California						
Labor Force Characteristics	State Population Total		Inside Metro Area		Outside Metro Area	
	Number	%	Number	%	Number	%
Employed Latinas over 16	1,232,502	20.0	1,203,503	97.6	28,999	2.4
Occupations						
Managerial & professional	187,150	15.2	182,606	15.2	4,544	15.7
Technical, sales, & admin. support	462,578	37.5	451,237	37.5	11,341	39.1
Service	288,003	23.4	281,082	23.4	6,921	23.9
Farming, forestry, & fishing	34,664	2.8	31,901	2.7	2,763	9.5
Precision, production, craft, & repair	49,310	4.0	48,737	4.0	573	2.0
Operators, fabricators, & laborers	210,797	17.1	207,940	17.3	2,857	9.9
Employment Sectors						
Agricultural	37,575	3.0				
Forestry & fisheries	532	0.1				
Mining	638	0.1				
Construction	13,828	1.1				
Manufacturing	250,027	20.3				
Transportation	45,116	3.7				
Wholesale	45,451	3.7				
Retail	214,381	17.4				
Finance	82,731	6.7				
Services	498,591	40.5				
Public Administration	43,632	3.5				

Source: U.S. Census Bureau: *1990 Census* (1993a)

Colorado						
Labor Force Characteristics	State Population Total		Inside Metro Area		Outside Metro Area	
	Number	%	Number	%	Number	%
Employed Latinas over 16	76,531	10.0	64,455	84.2	12,076	15.8
Occupations						
Managerial & professional	13,697	17.9	11,911	18.5	1,786	14.8
Technical, sales, & admin. support	30,841	40.3	26,831	41.6	4,010	33.2
Service	19,767	25.8	15,277	23.7	4,490	37.2
Farming, forestry, & fishing	577	0.8	307	0.5	270	2.2
Precision, production, craft, & repair	2,432	3.2	2,096	3.3	336	2.8
Operators, fabricators, & laborers	9,217	12.0	8,033	12.5	1,184	9.8
Employment Sectors						
Agricultural	511	0.7				
Forestry & fisheries	81	0.1				
Mining	376	0.5				
Construction	693	0.9				
Manufacturing	9,825	12.8				
Transportation	4,252	5.6				
Wholesale	2,008	2.6				
Retail	16,205	21.2				
Finance	5,278	6.9				
Services	32,880	43.0				
Public Administration	4,422	5.8				

Source: U.S. Census Bureau: *1990 Census* (1993a)

Florida						
Labor Force Characteristics	State Population Total		Inside Metro Area		Outside Metro Area	
	Number	%	Number	%	Number	%
Employed Latinas over 16	323,032	12.0	315,858	97.8	7,174	2.2
Occupations						
Managerial & professional	62,262	19.3	61,123	19.4	1,139	15.9
Technical, sales, & admin. support	145,759	45.1	143,375	45.4	2,384	33.2
Service	60,623	18.8	58,706	18.6	1,917	26.7
Farming, forestry, & fishing	6,487	2.0	5,437	1.7	1,050	14.6
Precision, production, craft, & repair	10,496	3.2	10,356	3.3	140	2.0
Operators, fabricators, & laborers	37,405	11.6	36,861	11.7	544	7.6
Employment Sectors						
Agricultural	7,129	2.2				
Forestry & fisheries	458	0.1				
Mining	98	0.1				
Construction	4,153	1.3				
Manufacturing	45,194	14.0				
Transportation	18,013	5.6				
Wholesale	16,441	5.1				
Retail	59,790	18.5				
Finance	34,107	10.6				
Services	128,107	39.6				
Public Administration	9,608	3.0				

Source: U.S. Census Bureau: *1990 Census* (1993a)

New Mexico						
Labor Force Characteristics	State Population Total		Inside Metro Area		Outside Metro Area	
	Number	%	Number	%	Number	%
Employed Latinas over 16	97,129	34.0	57,601	59.3	39,528	41
Occupations						
Managerial & rofessional	19,646	20.2	12,208	21.2	7,438	18.8
Technical, sales, & admin. support	42,197	43.4	25,938	45.0	16,259	41.1
Service	24,480	25.2	12,580	21.8	11,900	30.1
Farming, forestry, & fishing	704	0.8	477	0.8	227	0.7
Precision, production, craft, & repair	2,299	2.4	1,558	2.7	741	1.9
Operators, fabricators, & laborers	7,803	8.0	4,840	8.4	2,963	7.5
Employment Sectors						
Agricultural	843	0.9				
Forestry & fisheries	144	0.1				
Mining	218	0.2				
Construction	1,411	1.5				
Manufacturing	7,603	7.8				
Transportation	3,920	4.0				
Wholesale	1,431	1.5				
Retail	21,597	22.2				
Finance	6,315	6.5				
Services	44,696	46.0				
Public Administration	8,951	9.2				

Source: U.S. Census Bureau: *1990 Census* (1993a)

New York						
Labor Force Characteristics	State Population Total		Inside Metro Area		Outside Metro Area	
	Number	%	Number	%	Number	%
Employed Latinas over 16	355,854	9.0	352,174	99.0	3,680	1.0
Occupations						
Managerial & professional	65,861	18.5	64,954	18.4	907	24.6
Technical, sales, & admin. support	140,574	39.5	139,123	39.5	1,451	39.4
Service	81,669	23.0	80,778	22.9	891	24.2
Farming, forestry, & fishing	474	0.1	456	0.1	18	0.5
Precision, production, craft, & repair	10,616	3.0	10,564	3.0	52	1.4
Operators, fabricators, & laborers	56,660	15.9	56,299	16.0	361	9.8
Employment Sectors						
Agricultural	504	0.1				
Forestry & fisheries	28	0.0				
Mining	120	0.0				
Construction	3,034	0.9				
Manufacturing	68,480	19.2				
Transportation	16,248	4.6				
Wholesale	12,236	3.4				
Retail	44,997	12.6				
Finance	33,802	9.5				
Services	162,822	45.8				
Public Administration	13,583	3.8				

Source: U.S. Census Bureau: *1990 Census* (1993a)

Texas						
Labor Force Characteristics	State Population Total		Inside Metro Area		Outside Metro Area	
	Number	%	Number	%	Number	%
Employed Latinas over 16	664,428	20.0	579,361	87.2	85,067	12.8
Occupations						
Managerial & professional	111,788	16.8	99,943	17.3	11,845	13.9
Technical, sales, & admin. support	266,707	40.1	238,582	41.2	28,125	33.2
Service	181,554	27.3	150,516	26.0	31,038	36.5
Farming, forestry, & fishing	6,089	0.9	4,013	0.7	2,076	2.4
Precision, production, craft, & repair	19,847	3.0	17,430	3.0	2,417	2.8
Operators, fabricators, & laborers	78,443	11.8	68,877	11.9	9,566	11.2
Employment Sectors						
Agricultural	6,953	1.0				
Forestry & fisheries	130	0.0				
Mining	2,985	0.4				
Construction	6,339	1.0				
Manufacturing	81,931	12.3				
Transportation	23,513	3.5				
Wholesale	18,839	2.8				
Retail	150,823	22.7				
Finance	43,389	6.5				
Services	298,512	44.9				
Public Administration	31,014	4.7				

Source: U.S. Census Bureau: *1990 Census* (1993a)

APPENDIX C: Some Latina-Serving Programs in the United States

The Brotherhood/Sister Sol, New York, NY

The Brotherhood/Sister Sol describes itself as a "way of life" more than an organization. Founded in 1994 in Providence, Rhode Island, by two college seniors from Brown University, the Brotherhood/Sister Sol observes that it is the responsibility of older Black and Latino men to provide support to young males in their communities. Since its inception, seven chapters have been created in many communities in New York City, and in 1998, Susan Wilcox expanded the program to include "Sister Sol," a program for young Black and Latina women. Along with other goals, the Brotherhood/Sister Sol aspires to help youth develop into "empowered critical thinkers and leaders," to "develop a personal definition of brother/sister, man/woman, and leader that encompasses respect for themselves, their families, and the larger community," to broaden their understanding of social issues and their participation in their communities, to find their creative voices, and to gain a greater knowledge of their "historical inheritance as Black and Latino people." The organization's mission states that Black and Latino participants "live in war-torn communities where manhood is defined by abusive power and respect is synonymous with fear, and where women are bombarded with negative images of 'femininity' that have profound impacts on how they perceive themselves. Your young brothers and sisters are growing up in stressfully and challenging environments."

The Brotherhood/Sister Sol is composed of five programs: development, after-school, summer leadership, community outreach, and liberation. The program "recognizes [adolescents'] ability to decipher complex and socially relevant issues, and their desire to explore new ideas and experiences." The organization creates safe spaces for exploration of identity and beliefs, and support is available 24 hours a day, to "create a sense of family." Weekly meetings focus on critical thinking about issues such as "sexism and misogyny," sexual education and responsibility, conflict resolution, political education and citizenship, and service and responsibility. Summer leadership opportunities include a four-week summer study program in Latin America and Africa, employment training and paid internships, and camps. The "liberation" program contends that Black and Latino youth must "come to see themselves as leaders of today" rather than simply of the future. "It is essential they grasp the nature and roots of the problems in their communities, and develop strategies for improving the debilitating conditions surrounding them. In the communities where they live, it is not enough to attain individual success, although that too is critical, but to also work collectively toward bringing about ... change." The liberation program focuses on developing analytical skills, developing site visits and arranging briefings at local organizations, and developing organizational skills and experience in their community. Participants who complete the program become Brotherhood/Sister Sol "organizers" and receive a $500 honorarium.

A member praises the organization for teaching "how to fight society's discrimination, not in a violent way, but in pursuit of achieving my goals," and an East Side principal sees the organization as an "exceptionally valuable and irreplaceable part of school. I have witnessed incredible change and focus in our students. They have become aware and concerned about other young people and the devastating effects of racism in this society."

Contact: www.Brotherhood-Sistersol.org/
Box 11 Teachers College
Columbia University
New York NY 10027
212/678-3828

Latinas Somos, Chicago, IL

According to its website, the Latinas Somos Project works in the most disadvantaged barrios of Chicago, where young women have the least representation in social, economic, and political arenas. Within this context, Somos Latinas is bringing together two generations of Latinas to address these critical issues and change their communities. Its objectives are to develop Latina leaders within their own communities by fostering a commitment to social change; develop stable learning relationships between young Latinas and experienced Latina community organizers; and enhance the participation of young Latinas in the economic, educational, and political life of Chicago. Latinas Somos organizes "incubation" periods where mentors and mentorees get together informally to establish relationships based on interests. Thereafter, mentorees participate in weekly meetings to develop leadership skills; learn about community organizing; and discuss questions of sexuality, gender, and Latin American culture. Mentorees also intern with various community organizations to learn firsthand about being involved in the solution of community problems.

Contact: afscchicago@igc.apc.org
Elsa Chávez
American Friends Service Committee
59 E. Van Buren, Suite 1400
Chicago, IL 60605
312/427-2533

Leaders of a New Indiana (LONI), South Bend, IN

Through a grant from the Lilly Endowment, St. Mary's College in South Bend, Indiana—an all-women's Catholic college whose yearly tuition is $25,000—has developed an intensive and ambitious program to recruit and retain Latinas. The LONI project was "initiated to address the needs of two specific student populations in Indiana—those who were raised in communities of less than 25,000 and Latinas," according to *Hispanic Outlook*. The program targets these underrepresented groups in Indiana colleges because "both have strong family ties and values, and families they must leave in order to get a college education."

"We want young women to consider *all* of their possibilities," says Maria Thompson, director of the LONI project. "We want to make sure that they finish high school and contemplate the future." The project recognizes that "the road to college for Latinas is a journey that must begin early and include the support of family," according to *Hispanic Outlook*.

The initiative includes a two-week "Encuentro" program that invites high school Latinas to explore the possibilities for academic achievement and personal growth. Participants preview college life and courses in art, Latina literature, history, and computer science and are challenged to consider how they can identify and realize their goals.

LONI also includes the "My First Day of College" program, which allows first- and second-year high school students to preview college through a 24-hour stay on campus during which St. Mary's students act as hosts for social gatherings and classes. Prospective Latina students attend two workshops, one on admissions and one on navigating the financial aid process. The LONI project sponsors a one-week summer program on leadership development for pre-college Latinas that also invites parents to attend and learn more about educational options for their children.

St. Mary's admissions staff spend a lot of time doing intensive, face-to-face recruitment of potential Latina students. "The LONI project has enabled us to visit many high schools," says Mona Bowe, associate director of admissions, "but I am often out in the community talking to parents, grandparents, aunts, and uncles of potential Latina students because in this culture, the whole family is involved in the decision to attend college. ... If their daughter is going away to live on campus, they want to know how safe it is."

Once on campus, Latinas find student organizations and mentoring programs to cultivate success. La

Fuerza, a student organization with the slogan "because strength is feminine," has developed leadership roles by holding fundraisers, doing community service, and establishing a big sister/big brother program. "We nurture a closeness that is in line with what Latinas are used to in their families," explains Maria Oropeza, director of multicultural affairs.

Contact: www.saintmarys.edu/~loni/
219/284-4834

Source: Marilyn Gilroy, "Latinas Cultivated as Leaders of a New Indiana," *Hispanic Outlook in Higher Education*, February 11, 2000.

LLAMA: Latinas/Latinos Achieving More Academically, San Diego, CA

In 1989 a San Diego City School district evaluation found that Latinas showed the highest dropout rates and lowest achievement levels of any group in the district's schools. In 1992, based on these findings, a broad-based Latina Advocacy Program was formed. LLAMA promotes literacy and communication skills, high academic expectations, college, and positive school environment. Although initially focused on Latinas exclusively, it now services Latinos as well. LLAMA consists of "La Escuela," site-based programs for Latinas in 70 schools, and the "Bridges" program that connects Latino communities and San Diego city schools through referrals, volunteer recruitment and placement, joint projects, and mentorship projects. It also includes the "I Am, I Can/Soy y Puedo" initiative that links parents and students through workshops, educational opportunities, and intervention services, as well as special projects and assignments. The U.S. Forest Service, for example, sponsors an outdoor experience for 5th grade girls and literacy support. LLAMA cites as evidence of its impact the advancement in placement of Latina students from position #15 (1989) to position #10 (1996) by the school district's "16 Expectations" initiative, and the average of 70 percent enrollment in postsecondary education by those graduating seniors who participated in LLAMA Advocacy programs.

LLAMA identifies a lack of exposure to Latina role models in school, stereotypes of Latinas in the media and school, the number of Latinas referred to special education, and the lack of positive career counseling as probable factors contributing to the Latina dropout rate. Programs to celebrate Latina culture and expand Latinas' sense of possibilities include computer lab activities, skits and a Reader's Theater about important and influential Latinas, and assistance with study skills. A recent "Adelante Mujer Latina" conference brought Latinas together to consider their future academic options. Attendees commented positively that "the speakers talked truthfully and honestly," they "met professional Hispanic people," "everything talked about has something to do with our personal life," "the presenters encourage you to do what you most desire," and the result was "strong communication [among] Latinas."

Contact: San Diego City Schools/
LLAMA Advocacy Program
4606 Ingraham St.
San Diego, CA 92109
858/490-8689

MANA, A National Latina Organization, Washington, DC

MANA was founded in 1974 by a group of Mexican American women as the Mexican American Women's National Association. It became MANA in 1994, to reflect the growing diversity of the Latina population in the United States. MANA sponsors a national "hermanitas" program, a chapter-based initiative to address the needs of Hispanic girls. The program provides a comprehensive mind, body, and spirit approach to nurturing the development of young Latinas. Hermanitas emphasizes excellence in school by providing advanced education planning and career options, strengthened family units by engaging adults with young Latinas as mentors, and leadership through the creation of opportunities for service in the community. A major activity is the Annual National Hermanitas Summer Institute, a five-day leadership development conference that draws roughly 100 high school Latinas from around the nation.

Contact: www.hermana.org
1725 K St., NW, Suite 501
Washington, DC 20006
202/833-0060
hermana2@aol.com

Mary's Center for Maternal and Child Care, Washington, DC

Mary's Center was established in 1988 with joint funding from the D.C. Mayor's Office on Latino Affairs and the D.C. Commission of Public Health to address the demand for Spanish-speaking maternal and pediatric services in a predominately Latino area. The Center's mission is to provide holistic and culturally responsive health care to women and their families, recognizing the critical importance of the women's social environment and emotional well-being. A teen pregnancy prevention program has, according to the Center, been successful because it offers effective and affordable medical services, intensive follow-up, counseling, and an emphasis on both sexually active women and their partners ("it takes two to tango"). A case manager meets with the couple extensively to discuss birth control and to develop awareness of pregnancy prevention. The Center also has a male and a female case manager. Of 125 sexually active adolescents in the Teen Program at Mary's Center, 96 percent were not pregnant.

As part of its pregnancy prevention intervention program, Mary's Center has incorporated the "*Educación 2000*" program to improve academic achievement and prevent dropout among sexually active females. The program is a model of intervention that integrates students, parents, schools, and the community. Mary's Center has worked to integrate education as an important component of its pregnancy prevention intervention. Sexually active adolescents are at greater risk of dropping out of school than their non-sexually-active peers. Teens that set definite goals with their education are less likely to become teen parents. The education intervention at Mary's Center consists of after-school motivation and college preparation sessions, Saturday parent and student workshops, and intensive academic follow-up as needed. The program is being implemented in three local Washington, D.C., public schools as well.

Contact: www.maryscenter.org
Mary's Center for Maternal and Child Care
2333 Ontario Rd., NW
Washington, DC 20009
202/483-8196

Mi Carrera, Denver, CO

"Mi Carrera" is the second-oldest program of the Denver-based Mi Casa Resource Center for Women. It was initiated in 1979 as a four-year dropout prevention program for low-income girls attending the predominantly Hispanic West High School. Its dual goals are to reduce the dropout rate and increase the number of young Latina women who go on to college. Mi Carrera focuses on the development of life plans and self-exploration. Program options include leadership development, community activism, career awareness, computer classes, and workshops on a range of topics. Approximately 120 young women come through the program annually, with a core of 75, and in 1997 all of the participants graduated from high school. Ninety percent of those who graduated enrolled in college as first-generation students. Among its other highlights, Mi Carrera organizes an "options after high school" annual conference that brings together 200 young women from Denver high schools to meet with current college students, financial aid officers, and more than 20 college, trade school, and job recruiters. Former participant Felicia Lopez considers "the leaders and the other girls in the group to be my best friends. The women in Mi Carrera have motivated me to make something of myself."

Mi Casa also offers a program for pregnant or parenting teenage mothers who want to continue their education. It includes a 20-week GED preparation, life and parenting skills, and educational and career exploration program held twice a year.

Contact: www.micasadenver.org/carrera.htm
Mi Casa Resource Center for Women, Inc.
571 Galapago St.
Denver, CO 80204
303/573-1302

Mother-Daughter Programs: Tempe, AZ; El Paso, TX; Albuquerque, NM

Drawing on research that finds Hispanic mothers have a greater influence over their children than do Anglo mothers, some programs sponsored by colleges cultivate and develop the mother-daughter connection to promote academic identity.

In 1985 Jo Anne O'Donnell began the first mother-daughter program for Latinas at Arizona State University in Tempe. The program began with 25 teams of Hispanic mothers and 8th grade daughters from four middle schools in the Phoenix Elementary School District. Since then, the program has seen 739 mother-daughter teams through its 8th grade component, according to a 1995 review. The program aims to "excite Hispanic mothers and their daughters about the prospect of the girls attending college." Specifically, the program familiarizes at least 50 mother-daughter teams with higher education, encourages parental commitment to higher education, and helps Hispanic girls to make choices about their futures by familiarizing them with academic options. To qualify for the program students must be first-generation college candidates and demonstrate academic promise in school. The program begins in 8th grade but provides ongoing counseling and mentoring through high school and college. O'Donnell notes that the program has a "ripple effect—sometimes other family members look at education differently. They see a way out of the barrio, they see a way to another life."

A similar program at the University of Texas-El Paso (UTEP) targets girls entering the 6th grade who are nominated by teachers or principals because of their grades and test scores. The program encourages Hispanic girls to complete high school and includes counseling about professional career options. Like the ASU program, it offers tutoring and "big sisters" once Latinas enter UTEP. In addition to success with participating Latinas, the program has been successful for mothers as well. Originally the program's only goal for mothers was to teach them how to be good parents and role models, but organizer Josefina Tinajero found that "the mothers were hungry for information for themselves." Now the program has a Mothers' Initiative, whose goal is to "help mothers explore their own aspirations."

New Mexico State University's "*Generaciones*" program focuses on reducing high school dropout rates and boosting Latinas' college enrollment through university tours and volunteer help from "big sisters." *Generaciones* targets Latinas who fit at least three of the at-risk criteria for dropping out: those who come from single-parent families, those whose family income is less than $15,000 annually, those who are home alone for three or more hours a day, those whose parent/s have no high school diploma, those with "limited English proficiency," and those with a sibling who has dropped out of school. In some university tours, big sisters who are engineering students have demonstrated computer programs they have written themselves and introduced Latinas to mathematics, science, and computer science classrooms.

Source: María Luisa González et al., "Like Mother, Like Daughter: Intergenerational Programs for Hispanic Girls," *Educational Considerations*, 22 (2), Spring 1995.

ABOUT THE RESEARCHERS

Angela B. Ginorio

Angela B. Ginorio is associate professor of women's studies, and adjunct associate professor in the departments of psychology and American ethnic studies at the University of Washington in Seattle. She teaches courses on "Women and/in Science," "Issues for Ethnic Minorities and Women in Science and Engineering," "Gendered Technologies," and "Women and Violence."

Her scholarship focuses on factors affecting access to and experiences in science and engineering of underrepresented groups (students and faculty of color, women, students from rural backgrounds), with particular attention to the impact of socially defined identities, parental involvement, and mentoring. Her most recent publication on these topics is "The Transition to and from High School of Ethnic Minority Students" in G. Campbell, Jr., R. Denes & C. Morrison (eds.), *Access Denied: Race, Ethnicity, and the Scientific Enterprise* (New York: Oxford University Press, 2000). Other recent publications include "Feminism, Women's Studies and Engineering: Opportunities and Obstacles" in the *Journal of Women and Minorities in Science and Engineering* (with Banu Subramanian and Shirley Yee) and "The Feminist and the Scientist: One and the Same" (with Terry Marshall and Lisa Breckenridge).

She developed and directs the Rural Girls in Science Program of the University of Washington and received grants to support it from the National Science Foundation's Programs for Women and Girls, Microsoft, Alcoa, and the Discuren Foundation. She also does work on psychological issues for Latinas, and violence (with a focus on sexual harassment). On those topics her most recent publications are "Ethno-Race and Gender in Psychology: Where Are the Latinas?" co-authored with Lorraine Martinez and "Contextualizing Violence in a Participatory Classroom" (both in *Psychology of Women Quarterly*, Summer 1998).

She is a fellow of the American Psychological Association and the director of the Northwest Center for Research on Women until September 2000. She was raised and educated in Puerto Rico.

Michelle Huston

Michelle Huston is research coordinator for the Northwest Center for Research on Women (NWCROW) in Seattle. She holds a master's degree in sociology from the University of Washington, where she majored in gender and minored in statistics and methodology. At NWCROW, she has been responsible for evaluating the Rural Girls in Science project and consulted on the project's subsequent development. Her research interests focus on the educational paths taken by young women—especially girls from rural areas, first-generation college-bound girls, and girls who are ethnic minorities. She is also the founder of Chromazone, a research service for academic and business clients.

ENDNOTES

[1] For our own work in this and other papers, we prefer to use "Latina/o." For the sake of fidelity to the original source, when citing others' work we will use the term that most accurately describes the sample used by the authors.

[2] Puerto Rico's political status as a Commonwealth of the United States makes all Puerto Ricans citizens of the United States since 1917.

[3] Once in the United States, recent immigrants' experiences will be affected by their documentation status. Political refugees from Cuba and formerly from El Salvador receive different access to schooling, work, and health care possibilities than do Mexican nationals who remain undocumented in the United States when their entering visas expire or those who entered without legal documentation to begin with. Puerto Ricans, as citizens of the United States, in theory should receive all the benefits that citizens are entitled to. Undocumented people and their children have no legal access to education, legal work, and, to a large extent, health care. Estimates suggest that about 2.7 million undocumented individuals in the United States are from Mexico, 335,000 from El Salvador, and 165,000 from Guatemala (U.S. Immigration and Naturalization Service, www.ins.usdoj.gov/graphics/index.htm). Undocumented immigrants account for 1.9 percent of the total United States population, according to the INS.

[4] We provide little or no information about prekindergarten programs, distance learning, vocational training, and lifelong learning or continuing education. We also leave military training to other authors. Community-based learning through churches, the media, etc., is covered in the context of the learning that occurs within the community.

[5] For example, do we include everyone between the ages of 16 and 24? Only those ever enrolled in a U.S. school? Only those who register for the 9th grade?

[6] Although Latina, White, and Asian females are suspended at lower rates than their representation in the population, this is not true for African American females, who comprise 8 percent of the school population nationwide and contribute 10 percent of suspensions, a pattern evident on the state level as well (Office for Civil Rights: 1999).

[7] The "Texas Assessment of Academic Skills" (TAAS), a high-school level test required for graduation, has been touted as a system of accountability that is raising educational quality, especially for minority and underserved communities in the state. However, more research is required to understand how state systems of testing and test scores are related to actual learning and classroom practices. Some recent studies have investigated classroom practices and found that "test-prep activities are usurping a substantive curriculum" and diverting resources and attention from non-test related subjects (McNeil & Valenzuela: 2000).

[8] More research is required on how gender roles and expectations for males may affect their educational achievement. As shown this paper, Latinas are more likely to enter postsecondary education than Latinos, and also score higher on the NAEP, although lower on other standardized tests such as the SAT. Stanford University psychology professor Claude Steele has found that "academic disidentification" may account for poor educational outcomes among African

American males. Disidentification describes a process related to anxieties about stereotypes, whereby students withdraw from school. These students no longer derive self-esteem from educational achievement—they are neither disheartened by academic failure nor uplifted by academic success. A recent study applies the concept of academic disidentification and uses national data to compare grades, test scores, and self-esteem levels of African American, White, and Hispanic students in high school. This study finds that although academic disidentification was strong for African American males, it was not nearly as marked among African American females or Hispanic females. In fact, Latinas became "more invested" in their academics during high school, while Hispanic boys' investment dropped slightly. Although not as dramatic a drop as that noted for African American males, the finding suggests that Latinas experience more congruence between themselves and the schooling process than their male counterparts, but clearly less than their White female counterparts (Steele: 1997; Osborne: 1997).

BIBLIOGRAPHY

AAUW. (1991). *Shortchanging Girls, Shortchanging America.* Washington, DC.

AAUW Educational Foundation. (1998). *Gender Gaps: Where Schools Still Fail Our Children.* Washington, DC.

AAUW Educational Foundation. (1993). *Hostile Hallways: The AAUW Survey on Sexual Harassment in America's Schools.* Washington, DC.

AAUW Educational Foundation. (1992). *How Schools Shortchange Girls.* Washington, DC.

Abi-Mader, J. (1990, March). "A House for My Mother": Motivating Hispanic High School Students. *Anthropology and Education Quarterly,* 21, 41-58.

Adams, D., Astone, B., & Nunez-Wormack, E. (1994). Predicting the Academic Achievement of Puerto Rican and Mexican-American Ninth-Grade Students. *Urban Review,* 26, 1-14.

Adelman, C. (1999). *Answers in the Tool Box: Academic Intensity, Attendance Patterns and Bachelors Degree Attainment.* Washington, DC: U.S. Department of Education, Office of Educational Research and Improvement.

Alicea, I. P. (1994, January 1). Focus on the National Hispaña Leadership Institute. *Hispanic Outlook in Higher Education,* 4 (5), 6-7.

Alicea, I. P. (1997, September 19). No More Excuses: The Time to Act Is Now. *Hispanic Outlook in Higher Education,* 8 (2), 6.

American Council on Education. (1995). *Minorities in Higher Education Report 1994-1995.*

American Counseling Association. (1998). Developmental Career Programs for Schools, *ACA eNews* 1, 20. Available at www.counseling.org/enews/volume_1/0120a.htm.

Anzaldúa, G. (1987). *Borderlands: La Frontera—the New Mestiza.* San Francisco: Aunt Lute Books.

Aponte, R., & Siles, M. (1994). *Latinos in the Heartland: The Browning of the Midwest.* East Lansing, MI: Julian Samora Research Institute, Michigan State University. ERIC #ED414104.

Arbona, C., & Novy, D. M. (1991). Hispanic College Students: Are There Within-Group Differences? *Journal of College Student Development,* 32, 35-41.

Archer, J. (1996, March). Surge in Hispanic Enrollment Predicted, *Education Week [On-line serial],* 15 (27). Available at www.edweek.org/ew/vol-15/27census.h15

Arias, M. B. (1986). The Context of Education for Hispanic Students: An Overview. *The American Journal of Education,* 95, 26-57.

Aronson, E. (1999, November). The Power of Self Persuasion. *American Psychologist* 54 (11).

Azmitia, M., & Brown, J. R. (1999). *Continuity and Change in Latino Immigrant Parents' Beliefs About the "Path of Life."* Santa Cruz, CA: University of California.

Baldauf, S. (1997, August 20). Schools Try Tuning Into Latino Ways. *Christian Science Monitor.* Available at http://www.csmonitor.com/durable/1997/08/20/feat/learning.1.html.

Bennett, C. I., & Okinaka, A. (1990). Factors Related to Persistence Among Asians, Black, Hispanic, and White Undergraduates at a Predominantly White University: Comparison Between First and Fourth Year Cohorts. *The Urban Review,* 22, 33-60.

Bermúdez, A. B., & Prater, D. L. (1994). Examining the Effects of Gender and Second Language Proficiency on Hispanic Writers' Persuasive Discourse. *Bilingual Research Journal,* 18, 47-62.

Bernard, B. (1993). Fostering Resiliency in Kids. *Educational Leadership,* 51 (3), 44-48.

Bobo, M., Hildreth, B. L., & Durodoye, B. A. (1998). Changing Patterns in Career Choices Among African-American, Hispanic, and Anglo Children. *Professional School Counseling,* 1 (4), 37-42.

Boulón-Díaz, F. (1992). *The Effects of Intelligence on Social Class, Early Development and Pre-School Experience on School Achievement of Puerto Rican School Children.* Paper presented at the Annual Convention of the American Psychological Association, Washington, DC. August 14-18.

Bressler, S. (1996). Voices of Latina Migrant Mothers in Rural Pennsylvania. In Judith Leblanc Flores (ed.). *Children of La Frontera: Binational Efforts to Service Mexican Migrant and Immigrant Students.* Washington, DC. ERIC #ED393647.

Brooks, A. J., Stuewig, J., & LeCrow, C. W. (1998). Family Based Model of Hispanic Adolescent Substance Use. *Journal of Drug Education,* 28 (1), 65-86.

Brown, F., & Stent, M. D. (1977). *Minorities in U.S. Institutions of Higher Education.* New York: Praeger.

Brown, L. M. (1998). Ethnic Stigma as a Contextual Experience: A Possible Selves Perspective. *PSPS,* 24 (2), 163-172.

Brown, S. V. (2000). The Preparation of Minorities for Academic Careers in Science and Engineering: How Well Are We Doing? In G. Campbell, Jr., R. Penes, & C. Morrison (eds.) *Access Denied: Race, Ethnicity, and the Scientific Enterprise.* New York: Oxford University Press.

Bruno, J. E. (1983). Equal Education Opportunity and Declining Teacher Morale at Black, White, and Hispanic High Schools in a Large Urban School District. *The Urban Review,* 15 (1), 19-36.

Burke, D. J. (1995). Hispanic Youth and the Secondary School Culture. *The High School Journal,* 78, 185-194.

California State Department of Education. (1981). *Schooling and Language Minority Students: A Theoretical Framework.* Los Angeles: Evaluation, Dissemination and Assessment Center.

Cantú, M. (2000). *Attitudes of Receiving Teachers and Educational Success of Migrant Students.* Paper presented at the Annual Meeting of the American Educational Research Association, New Orleans, LA. April 24-28.

Capello, D. C. (1994). Beyond Financial Aid: Counseling Latina Students. *Journal of Multicultural Counseling and Development,* 22 (1), 28-36.

Cardoza, D. (1991). College Attendance and Persistence Among Hispanic Women: An Examination of Some Contributing Factors. *Sex Roles,* 7 (3/4), 147-165.

Castellanos, M., & Fujitsubo, L. C. (1997). Academic Success Among Mexican American Women in a Community College. *Community College Journal of Research and Practice,* 21 (8), 695-708.

Castillo-Speed, L., (ed.). (1995). *Latina: Women's Voices from the Borderlands.* New York: Simon & Schuster.

Castro, I. (2000). *Latinas/Latinos Achieving More Academically (LLAMA) Advocacy Program.* Paper presented at the "Urban Girls: Entering the New Millennium" conference. Buffalo, NY. April 14-15.

Centers for Disease Control and Prevention (1998). Youth Risk Behavior Surveillance—United States, 1997, *MMWR,* 73.

Chacón, M. A., Cohen, E. G., Camarena, M. M., Gonzáles, J. T., & Strover, S. (1983, Winter). Chicanas in California Post Secondary Education. *La Red/The Net,* Supplement no. 65.

Chacón, M. A. et al. (1982). *Chicanas in Postsecondary Education.* Stanford, CA: Center for Research on Women. ERIC #ED223186.

Chesney-Lind, M., & Hagedorn, J. K. (1999). Just Every Mother's Angel: An Analysis of Gender and Ethnic Variations in Youth Gang Membership. In M. Chesney-Lind & J. Hagedorn (eds.). *Female*

Gangs in America: Essays on Girls, Gangs, and Gender. Chicago: Lake View Press.

Clewell, B. C., & Braddock, J. H., II (2000). Influences on Minority Participation in Mathematics, Science, and Engineering. In G. Campbell, Jr., R. Denes, & C. Morrison (eds.). *Access Denied: Race, Ethnicity, and the Scientific Enterprise* (pp. 89-137). New York: Oxford University Press.

Cohen, J., Blanc, S., with Christman, J., Brown, D., & Sims, M. (1996). *Girls in the Middle: Working to Succeed in School.* Washington, DC: American Association of University Women Educational Foundation.

College Board, Advanced Placement Program. (1999). *National Total: AP Grade Distributions by Total and Ethnic Group, Males and Females.* New York.

College Board. (1999a). *1999 Profile of College Bound Seniors—SAT Mean Scores and Standard Deviations for Males, Females, and Total by Ethnic Group.* New York.

College-Bound Hispanics: Marking the Path. (1998, February). *Hispanic Outlook in Higher Education* 8 (11), 3.

Collins, W. A., Maccoby, E. E., Steinberg, L., Hetherington, E. M., & Bornstein, M. H. (2000). Contemporary Research on Parenting. *American Psychologist,* 55 (2), 218-232.

Commonwealth Fund. (1997). *The Commonwealth Fund Survey of the Health of Adolescent Girls.* New York.

Coombs, R. H., Paulson, M. J., & Richardson, M. A. (1991). Peer vs. Parental Influence in Substance Use Among Hispanic and Anglo Children and Adolescents. *Journal of Youth and Adolescence,* 20, 73-88.

Cornwell, T. (1998, July 10). Hispanic Hothouse in Vegas. *The Times Higher Education Supplement,* 1340, 12.

Cross, S. E., & Markus, H. R. (1994). Self-Schemas, Possible Selves, and Competent Performance. *Journal of Educational Psychology,* 86 (3), 423-438.

Dabul, A. J., & Russo, N. F. (1996). Rethinking Psychological Theory to Encompass Issues of Gender and Ethnicity: Focus on Achievement. In K. F. Wyche & F. J. Crosby (eds.). *Women's Ethnicities: Journeys through Psychology.* Boulder, CO: Westview Press.

Darden, J. T., Bagakás, J. G., & Armstrong, T. (1994, December). The Segregation of Undergraduate Hispanic Students in United States Institutions of Higher Education. *Equity and Excellence in Education,* 27, 69-75.

Davenport, E. C., Jr., Davidson, M. L., & Kuang, J. (1998). High School Mathematics Course-taking by Gender and Ethnicity. *American Educational Research Journal,* 35 (3), 497-514.

Day, J. D., Borkowski, J. G., Punzo, D., & Howsepian, B. (1994). Enhancing Possible Selves in Mexican American Students. *Motivation and Emotion,* 18 (1), 79-103.

De Acosta, M. (1993). *The Cleveland Hispanic Community and Education: A Struggle for Voice.* Occasional Paper #9. Cleveland, OH: Urban Child Research Center, Cleveland State University. ERIC #ED361454.

DeBlassie, A. M., & DeBlassie, R. D. (1996, Spring). Education of Hispanic Youth: A Cultural Lag. *Adolescence,* 31, 205-216.

De las Fuentes, C., & Vásquez, M. J. T. (1999). American-Born Asian, African, Latina, and American Indian Adolescent Girls: Challenges and Strengths. In N. G. Johnson, M. Roberts & J. Whorell (eds.). *Adolescent Girls: Strengths and Stresses* (pp. 151-173). Washington, DC: American Psychological Association.

Del Pinal, J., & Singer, A. (1997). Generations of Diversity: Latinos in the United States. *Population Bulletin,* 52 (3), 1-48.

Delgado-Gaitan, C. (1991). Involving Parents in Schools: A Process of Empowerment. *American Journal of Education* 100 (1), 20-46.

Dietrich, L. C. (1998). *Chicana Adolescents. Bitches, 'Ho's', and Schoolgirls.* Westport, CT: Praeger.

Dozier, A. L., & Barnes, M. J. (1997, Winter). Ethnicity, Drug User Status and Academic Performance. *Adolescence,* 32, 825-37.

Durán, R. (1983). *Hispanics' Education and Background: Predictors of College Achievement.* New York: The College Board.

Durán, R. (2000). *Latino Immigrant Parents and Children Learning and Publishing Together in an After School Setting.* Paper presented at the Annual Meeting of the American Educational Research Association, New Orleans, LA. April 24-28.

Educational Testing Service. (1998). *Order in the Classroom: Violence, Discipline, and Student Achievement.* Princeton, NJ.

Erickson, P. (1998). *Latina Adolescent Childbearing in East Los Angeles.* Austin, TX: University of Texas Press.

Eschbach, K., & Gómez, C. (1998). Choosing Hispanic Identity: Ethnic Identity Switching Among Respondents to High School and Beyond. *Social Science Quarterly,* 79 (1), 74-90.

Esparanza, S. (1996, September 15). Education: Michigan's Hispanics Outperform National Counterparts Academically, Census Shows. *The Detroit News and Free Press.* A, 14:1

Espín, O. M., & Goodenow, C. (1993). Identity Choices in Immigrant Adolescent Females. *Adolescence,* 28 (109), 173-184.

Fairchild, H. (1989). School Size, Per Pupil Expenditure, and Academic Achievement. *Review of Public Data Use,* 12, 221-229.

Farmer, H. S., Wardrop, J. L., & Rotella, S. C. (1999). Antecedent Factors Differentiating Women and Men in Science/Nonscience Careers. *Psychology of Women Quarterly,* 23, 763-780.

Fine, M. (1991). *Framing Dropouts: Notes on the Politics of an Urban Public High School.* Albany, NY: SUNY Press.

Fine, M., & Weis, L. (eds.) (1998). *The Unknown City: The Lives of Poor and Working-Class Young Adults.* Boston: Beacon Press.

Flores-Niemann, Y., Romero, A., & Arbona, C. (2000, February). Effects of Cultural Orientation on the Perception of Conflict between Relationship and Education Goals for Mexican American College Students. *Hispanic Journal of Behavioral Sciences,* 22 (1) 46-63.

Fordham, S. (1996). *Blacked Out: Dilemmas of Race, Identity, and Success at Capital High.* Chicago: University of Chicago Press.

Forste, R., & Tienda, M. (1992). Race and Ethnic Variation in the Schooling Consequences of Female Adolescent Sexual Activity. *Social Science Quarterly,* 73 (1), 12-30.

Fuentes, E. G., & LeCapitaine, J. E. (1990, Spring). The Effects of a Primary Prevention Program on Hispanic Children. *Education,* 110, 298-303.

Fuentes, L. (1994). Educating Puerto Ricans in the U.S.: The Struggle for Equity. *Equity and Excellence in Education,* 27 (1), 16-19.

Fuertes, J. N., & Sedlacek, W. E. (1994, September). Predicting the Academic Success of Hispanic College Students using SAT Scores. *College Student Journal,* 28, 350-352.

Fuller, B., Eggers-Piérola, C., Holloway, S. D., Liang, X., & Rambaud, M. F. (1996). Rich Culture, Poor Markets: Why Do Latino Parents Forgo Preschool? *Teachers College Record,* 97 (3), 400-418.

Gándara, P. (1995). *Over the Ivy Walls: The Educational Mobility of Low-Income Chicanas.* Albany, NY: State University of New York Press.

García & Associates. (1998, February 27). Cited in "Why Hispanic American Women Succeed in Higher Education." *Hispanic Outlook in Higher Education,* 12.

Genesee, F. (1999). *Program Alternatives for Linguistically Diverse Students.* Educational Practices Report 1, Center for Research on Education, Diversity and Excellence, Santa Cruz, CA. Washington, DC: Office of Educational Research and Improvement.

Genesee, F., & P. Gándara (1999, Winter). Bilingual Education Programs: A Cross-National Perspective. *Journal of Social Issues*.

Giloy, M. (1999, December 17). Gap Remains in Minority SAT Scores. *Hispanic Outlook in Higher Education*, 28-30.

Ginorio, A. B. (1996). A Culture of Meaningful Community. In *Bridging the Gender Gap in Engineering and Science: The Challenge of Institutional Transformation, Special Report* (pp. 29-32). Available from Carnegie Mellon University, 5000 Forbes Ave. WH 419, Pittsburgh, PA 15213.

Ginorio, A. B., & Grignon, J. (2000). The Transition To and From High School of Ethnic Minority Students. In G. Campbell, Jr., R. Denes, & C. Morrison (eds.). *Access Denied: Race, Ethnicity, and the Scientific Enterprise* (pp. 151-173). New York: Oxford University Press.

Ginorio, A. B., Gutiérrez, L., Cauce, A. M., & Acosta, M. (1995). Psychological Issues for Latinas. In H. Landrine (ed.). *Bringing Cultural Diversity to Feminist Psychology* (pp. 241-263). Washington, DC: American Psychological Association.

Ginorio, A. B., & Huston, M. (2000, Spring). Latina Focus Group. Unpublished raw data.

Ginorio, A. B., & Marshall, T. (in progress). *Longitudinal Assessment of Participants in the Rural Girls in Science Program*.

Ginorio, A. B., & Martínez, L. J. (1998). Where Are the Latinas? Ethno-Race and Gender in Psychology Courses. *Psychology of Women Quarterly*, 22, 53-68.

Gloria, A. M. (1997). Chicana Academic Persistence: Creating a University-Based Community. *Education and Urban Society*, 30 (1), 107-121.

Goldenberg, C. (1987). Low-Income Hispanic Parents' Contributions to their First-Grade Children's Word-Recognition Skills. *Anthropology and Education Quarterly* 18 (3), 149-79.

Gómez, M. J., & Fassinger, R. E. (1994). An Initial Model of Latina Achievement: Acculturation, Biculturalism, and Achieving Styles. *Journal of Counseling Psychology*, 41 (2), 205-215.

Gómez, M. J., & Fassinger, R. E. (2000). *Career Paths of Highly Accomplished Latinas*. Paper presented at the Annual Meeting of the American Psychological Association, New York. August 4-8.

González, G. M. (1990). A Comparison of Alcohol Use and Alcohol-Related Problems Among Caucasian, Black, and Hispanic College Students. *NASPA Journal*, 17, 330-335.

González, S. T. (1988). Dilemmas of the High-Achieving Chicana: The Double-Bind Factor in Male/Female Relationships. *Sex Roles*, 18, 367-380.

Guerra, J. C. (1996). "It Is As If My Story Repeats Itself." Life, Language, and Literacy in Chicago Communidad. *Education and Urban Society*, 29 (1), 35-53.

Haag, P. (1999). *Voices of a Generation: Teenage Girls on Sex, School, and Self*. Washington, DC: American Association of University Women Educational Foundation.

Haas, N. S., & Sullivan, H. J. (1991, July). Use of Ethnically Matched Role Models in Career Materials for Hispanic Students. *Contemporary Educational Psychology*, 16, 272-278.

Harris, M. G. (1988). *Cholas: Latina Girls and Gangs*. New York: AMS Press.

Headden, S. (1997, October 20). The Hispanic Dropout Mystery. *U.S. News and World Report*. Available at *www.usnews.com/usnews/issue/971020/20hisp.htm*.

Hernández, A. E. (1995, Fall). Enhancing the Academic Success of Hispanic Females (Hispanic Mother-Daughter Program of Texas). *Contemporary Education*, 67, 18-20.

Hickey, M. G. (1998). "Back Home, Nobody'd Do That": Immigrant Students and Cultural Models of Schooling (With Emphasis on Asian and Hispanic Children). *Social Education*, 62 (7), 442-447.

Hispanic Children Are Less Well-Educated and More Likely to Drop Out. (1985, November). *Phi Delta Kappan,* 67, 242.

Holman, L. J. (1997, April). Working Effectively with Hispanic Immigrant Families. *Phi Delta Kappan,* 78, 647-649.

Huston, M., Ginorio, A., Frevert, K., and Bierman, J. (1996). *Final Report to the Program for Women and Girls at the National Science Foundation.* Available from the National Science Foundation or Rural Girls in Science, Box 353180, University of Washington, Seattle, WA 98195.

Jacobson, L. (1998). Hispanic Children Outnumber Young Blacks for the First Time. *Education Week,* 17 (43), 6.

Johnston, R. C., & Viadero, D. (2000). Unmet Promise: Raising Minority Achievement. *Education Week,* 19 (27), 1.

Jones, T. G. (1995, January). A Framework for Investigating Minority Group Influence in Urban School Reform. *Urban Education,* 29, 375-395.

Jones-Correa, M., & Leal, D. L. (1996). Becoming "Hispanic": Secondary Panethnic Identification Among Latin American-Origin Populations in the United States. *Hispanic Journal of Behavioral Sciences,* 18 (2), 214-254.

Kahn, J., & Berkowitz, R. (1995). *Sources of Support for Young Latina Mothers.* Washington, DC: The Urban Institute.

Kane, M., & Pelavin, S. (1990). *Changing the Odds: Factors Increasing Access to College.* New York: The College Board.

Kann, L. K., Kinchen, S. A., & Williams, B. L. (1998, November). Youth Risk Behavior Surveillance—United States, 1997. *The Journal of School Health,* 68 (9), 355-69.

Kaplan, C. (1990). *Critical Factors Affecting School Dropout Among Mexican-American Women.* Los Angeles: University of California, Los Angeles.

Katz, S. R. (1996). Where the Streets Cross the Classroom: A Study of Latino Students' Perspectives on Cultural Identity in City Schools and Neighborhood Gangs. *Bilingual Research Journal,* 20, 603-631.

Kaufman, P., Kwon, J. Y., & Klein, S. (1999). *Dropout Rates in the United States: 1998.* Washington, DC: National Center for Education Statistics.

Kinard, B., & Bitter, G. G. (1997). Multicultural Mathematics and Technology: The Hispanic Math Project. *Computers in the Schools,* 13 (1-2), 77-88.

Kitano, M. (1998, Winter). Gifted Latina Women. *Journal for the Education of the Gifted,* 21, 131-159.

Lango, D. R. (1995). Mexican American Female Enrollment in Graduate Programs: A Study of the Characteristics That May Predict Success. *Hispanic Journal of Behavioral Sciences,* 17 (1), 33-48.

Latino Coalition for a Healthy California. (2000). *Policy Development and Advocacy: Fact Sheet-Demographics. A Latino Sociodemographic Profile.* Available at www.lchc.org/policy/demo.htm.

Lauver, P. J., & Jones, R. M. (1991, April). Factors Associated with Perceived Career Options in American Indian, White, and Hispanic Rural High School Students. *Journal of Counseling Psychology,* 38, 159-166.

LaVelle, M. (1996). *The Importance of Learning English: A National Survey of Hispanic Parents.* Washington, DC: Center for Equal Opportunity. ERIC #ED405726.

The Learning Curve: UTSA Gets High Marks. (1997, May 13). *The San Antonio Express-News Online.* Available at http://www.mysanantonio.com/

Lee, V. (1988). Achievement and Educational Aspirations Among Hispanic Female High School Students: Comparison Between Public and Catholic Schools. In F. Press (ed.). *The Broken Web* (pp. 179-192). Encino, CA: Floricanto Press.

Levine, A., & Nidiffer, J. (1996). *Beating the Odds: How the Poor Get to College.* San Francisco: Jossey-Bass.

Lindberg, L. D., Boggess, S., Porter, L., & Williams, S. (2000). *Teen Risk-Taking: A Statistical Report.* Washington, DC: Urban Institute.

Lockwood, A. T., & Secada, W. G. (2000). *Transforming Education for Hispanic Youth: Exemplary Practices, Programs, and Schools.* Washington, DC: National Clearinghouse for Bilingual Education.

López, C., & Sullivan, H. (1992). Effect of Personalization of Instructional Context on the Achievement and Attitudes of Hispanic Students. *Educational Technology Research and Development* 40 (4), 5-13.

López, E. M. (1995). Challenges and Resources of Mexican American Students within the Family, Peer Group, and University: Age and Gender Patterns. *Hispanic Journal of Behavioral Sciences,* 17 (4), 499-508.

Luker, K. (1997). Dubious Conceptions: The Politics of Teenage Pregnancy. Cambridge, MA: Harvard University Press.

Lynch, E. W., & Stein, R. C. (1987, October). Parent Participation By Ethnicity: A Comparison of Hispanic, Black, and Anglo Families. *Exceptional Children,* 54, 105-111.

Manlove, J. (1998). The Influence of High School Dropout and School Disengagement on the Risk of School-Age Pregnancy. *Journal of Research on Adolescence,* 8 (2), 187-220.

Markus, H., & Nurius, P. (1986). Possible Selves. *American Psychologist,* 41 (9), 954-969.

Martínez, Y. G., Scott, J., Jr., Cranston-Gingras, A., & Platt, J. S. (1994, Winter). Voices from the Field: Interviews with Students from Migrant Farmworker Families. *The Journal of Educational Issues of Language Minority Students,* 14, 333-348.

Matute-Bianchi, A., & E. M. (1986, November). Ethnic Identities and Patterns of School Success and Failure Among Mexican-Descent and Japanese-American Students in a California High School. *American Journal of Education,* 95, 233-255.

Maxwell, M. P., Maxwell, J. D., & Krugly-Smolska, E. (1996, Summer). Ethnicity, Gender and Occupational Choices in Two Toronto Schools. *Canadian Journal of Education,* 21, 257-279.

McCool, A. C. (1984, Spring). Improving the Admission and Retention of Hispanic Students—A Dilemma for Higher Education. *College Student Journal,* 18, 28-36.

McNeil, L., & Valenzuela, A. (2000) The Harmful Impact of the TAAS System of Testing in Texas: Beneath the Accountability Rhetoric. Cambridge, MA: Harvard University, The Civil Rights Project. Available at www.law.harvard.edu/civilrights/conferences/testing98/mcneil_valenzuela.html.

Meek, A. (1998, February). America's Teachers: Much to Celebrate. *Educational Leadership,* 55, 12-16.

Mellander, G. (1998, February 13). College-Bound Hispanics. *Hispanic Outlook in Higher Education,* 8 (12) 12.

Mellander, G. (2000, February 11). The Digital Divide and Hispanics. *Hispanic Outlook in Higher Education,* 10 (10) 5.

Miramontes, O. B. (1990). A Comparative Study of English Oral Reading Skills in Differently Schooled Groups of Hispanic Students. *Journal of Reading Behavior,* 22 (4), 373-394.

Miranda, A. O., & Umhoefer, D. L. (1998, January). Acculturation, Language Use, and Demographic Variables as Predictors of the Career Self-efficacy of Latino Career Counseling Clients. *Journal of Multicultural Counseling and Development,* 26, 39-51.

Monsivais, G. I. (1990). *Latino Teachers: Well Educated but Not Prepared: An Executive Summary.* Claremont, CA: Tomas Rivera Center.

Morse, S. (2000, Fall). A Foot in Two Worlds: Latinas in School Today. *AAUW Outlook,* 94(2), 36-39.

Mortenson, T. G. (2000). Financing Opportunity for Postsecondary Education. In G. Campbell, Jr., R. Denes, & C. Morrison (eds.). *Access Denied: Race,*

Ethnicity, and the Scientific Enterprise (pp. 221-236). New York, Oxford University Press.

Muñoz, V. I. (1995). *Where "Something Catches."* Albany, NY: State University of New York Press.

National Science and Technology Council. (2000). *Ensuring a Strong U.S. Scientific, Technical, and Engineering Workforce in the 21st Century.* Washington, DC.

Nevárez-La Torre, A. A., & Hidalgo, N. M. (1997, November). Latino Communities: Resources for Educational Change (Introduction). *Education and Urban Society,* 30, 3-19.

Oakes, J. (1990). *Lost Talent: The Underparticipation of Women, Minorities, and Disabled Persons in Science.* Santa Monica, CA: RAND Publications Series.

Office for Civil Rights. (1999). *1997 Elementary and Secondary School Civil Rights Compliance Report: National and State Projections.* Washington, DC.

O'Halloran, C. S. (1995). Mexican American Female Students Who Were Successful in High School Science Courses. *Equity & Excellence in Education,* 28 (2), 57-64.

Ohye, B. Y., & Daniel, J. H. (1997). Adolescent Girls and Media Images of Womanhood: Who Will I Be When I Grow Up? In N.G. Johnson, M. Robens, & J. Worell (eds.), *Beyond Appearance: A New Look at Adolescent Girls.* Washington, DC: ADA.

Olivas, M. A. (ed.). (1986). *Latino College Students.* New York: Teachers College, Columbia University.

On Many Edges: The Hispanic Population of Indiana. (1996). Hammond, IN: Heartland Center Reports. ERIC #ED406077. Available at www.thetimesonline.com/org/Heartland/hispanic.html.

Orenstein, P., in association with the American Association of University Women. (1994). *School Girls: Young Women, Self-Esteem, and the Confidence Gap.* New York: Doubleday.

Ortiz, V. (1997). Family Economic Strategies Among Latinas. *Race, Gender and Class,* 4 (2), 91-106.

Osborne, J. (1997, December). Race and Academic Disidentification. *Journal of Educational Psychology,* 89, 728-735.

Oyserman, D. (1990). Possible Selves in Balance: Implications for Delinquency. *Journal of Social Issues* 36 (2), 141-57.

Oyserman, D., Ager, J., & Gant, L. (1995). A Socially Contextualized Model of African American Identity: Possible Selves and School Persistence. *Journal of Personality and Social Psychology,* 69 (6), 1216-1232.

Padilla, A. M., Fairchild, H., & Valadex, C. M. (eds.). (1990). *Bilingual Education: Issues and Strategies.* Newbury Park, CA: Sage Publications.

Paratore, J., et al (1999). Discourse Between Teachers and Latino Parents During Conferences Based on Home Literacy Portfolios. *Education and Urban Society* 32 (1), 58-82.

Patthey-Chávez, G. G. (1993). High School as an Area for Cultural Conflict and Acculturation for Latino Angelinos. *Anthropology and Education Quarterly,* 24 (1), 33-60.

Pérez, G. V. (2000). *The Challenge of Migrant Student Identification.* Paper presented at the Annual Meeting of the American Educational Research Association, New Orleans, LA. April 24-28.

Perna, L. W. (2000). *Racial/Ethnic Group Differences in the Realization of Educational Plans.* Paper presented at the Annual Meeting of the American Educational Research Association, New Orleans, LA. April 24-28.

Phillips, L. (1998). *The Girls Report: What We Know and Need to Know about Growing Up Female.* New York: National Council for Research on Women.

Pomales, J., & Williams, V. (1989, January). Effects of Level of Acculturation and Counseling Style on Hispanic Students' Perceptions of Counselors. *Journal of Counseling Psychology,* 36, 79-83.

Portillos, E. L. (1999). The Social Construction of Gender in the Barrio. In M. Chesney-Lind & J. Hagedorn (eds.). *Female Gangs in America: Essays* on *Girls, Gangs, and Gender.* Chicago: Lake View Press.

Portner, J. (1998, February 25). Hispanic Teenagers Top Black, White Birthrates. *Education Week,* 17, 5.

President's Advisory Commission on Educational Excellence for Hispanic Americans. (1996). *Our Nation on the Fault Line: Hispanic American Education.* Washington, DC.

Quiroz, B., Marks, P., & Altchech, M. (1999). Bridging Culture with a Parent-Teacher Conference. *Educational Leadership,* 56 (7), 68-70.

Race Theory Gets Cool Reception (Success of Asian Students Compared to Whites, Blacks, and Hispanics). (1989, February 10). *The Times Higher Education Supplement,* 10, N849.

Ramos-Zayas, A. Y. (1998). Nationalist Ideologies, Neighborhood-Based Activism, and Educational Spaces in Puerto Rican Chicago. *Harvard Educational Review,* 68 (2), 164-192.

Rendón, L. I., & Amaury, N. (1987). Hispanic Students: Stopping the Leaks in the Pipeline. *Educational Record,* 68/69, 79-85.

Rendón, L. I., & Amaury, N. (1989, Summer). A Synthesis and Application of Research on Hispanic Students in Community College. *Community College Review,* 17, 17-24.

Reyes, O., & Jason, L. A. (1993). Pilot Study Examining Factors Associated with Academic Success for Hispanic High School Students. *Journal of Youth and Adolescence,* 22 (1), 57-71.

Rich, L. & Kim, S. (1999). Patterns of Later Life Education Among Teenage Mothers. *Gender and Society,* 13 (6), 798-817.

Riley Cites Hispanic Education Needs. (1999, July 16). *Education Week.*

Rodríguez, C. (1993). *Minorities in Science and Engineering: Patterns for Success.* Tucson, AR: University of Arizona, Tucson.

Rodríguez, C. (2000, March). Personal communication.

Rodríguez, P., & Crocker, E. V. (1992). *In Search of Economic Equity.* Washington, DC: MANA.

Romo, H. D., & Falbo, T. (1996). *Latino High School Graduation.* Austin, TX: University of Texas Press.

Rumbaut, R. (1994). The Crucible Within: Ethnic Identity, Self-Esteem, and Segmented Assimilation Among Children of Immigrants. *International Migration Review,* 28 (4), 748-794.

Rumbaut, R. G. (1996). *Immigrants from Latin America and the Caribbean: A Socioeconomic Profile.* East Lansing, MI: Julian Samora Research Institute. ERIC #ED4131357.

Rumberger, R. W., & Larson, K. A. (1998). Toward Explaining Differences in Educational Achievement Among Mexican American Language-Minority Students. *Sociology of Education,* 71, 68-92.

Salgado de Snyder, N.S., Cervantes, R.C., & Padilla, A.M. (1990). Gender and Ethnic Differences in Psychological Stress and Generalized Distress Among Hispanics. *Sex Roles: A Journal of Research,* 22 (7-8), 441-453.

Sánchez, J. E., Marder, F., & Berry, R. (1992, Winter). Dropping Out: Hispanic Students, Attrition, and the Family. *College and University,* 67, 145-150.

San Diego City Schools. (2000). *Data Comparison 1986-2000 (7th-12th Grades): Dropout and School Population by Race and Ethnicity.* San Diego, CA: LLAMA Advocacy Program.

San Diego City Schools, Planning, Research, and Evaluation Division. (1989). *Empowering the Hispanic Female in the Public School Setting, Part II.* San Diego, CA: City School District.

Sarracent, M. C. (1999, April 23). Latinas Speak Out at Princeton University Roundtable. *Hispanic Outlook in Higher Education,* 40-43.

Schmitt, A. P. (1988, Spring). Language and Cultural Characteristics that Explain Differential Item

Functioning for Hispanic Examinees on the Scholastic Aptitude Test. *Journal of Educational Measurement,* 25, 1-13.

Schnaiberg, L. (1998, February 11). U.S. Report Tracks High Dropout Rate Among Hispanics. *Education Week,* 7.

Scott, M. S., Perou, R., & Urbano, R. C. (1992, Summer). The Identification of Giftedness: A Comparison of White, Hispanic and Black Families. *Gifted Child Quarterly,* 36, 131-139.

Secada, W. G., Chávez-Chávez, R., García, E., Muñoz, C., Oakes, J., Santiago-Santiago, I., & Slavin, R. (1998). *No More Excuses: The Final Report of the Hispanic Dropout Project.* Washington, DC: U.S. Department of Education, Office of Bilingual and Minority Languages Affairs.

Seymour, E., & Hewitt, N. M. (1997). *Talking About Leaving: Why Undergraduates Leave the Sciences.* Boulder, CO: Westview Press.

Shanahan, T., Mulhern, M., & Rodríguez-Brown, F. V. (1995, April). Project FLAME: Lessons Learned from a Family Literacy Program for Linguistic Minority Families. Family Literacy: Aprendiendo, Mejorando, Educando (Learning, Bettering, Educating) in Chicago. *The Reading Teacher,* 48, 586-593.

Sheets, R. H. (1995). From Remedial to Gifted: Effects of Culturally Centered Pedagogy. *Theory into Practice,* 34 (3), 390-396.

Shivley, T. E. (2000). *High Trust, High-Involvement Culture: To Act, To Give, To Risk—A Paradigm for Student Voice in Educational Reform.* Paper presented at the Annual Meeting of the American Educational Research Association, New Orleans, LA. April 24-28.

Smart, J. F., & Smart, D. W. (1995, March/April). Acculturative Stress of Hispanics: Loss and Challenge. *Journal of Counseling and Development,* 73, 390-396.

Smith, T. M. (1995). The Educational Progress of Hispanic Students. In A. Livingston & S. Miranda (eds.). *The Condition of Education 1995,* 4. Washington, DC: U.S. Department of Education, Office of Educational Research and Improvement, National Center for Education Statistics, Data Development Division.

So, A.Y. (1984, July). The Financing of College Education by Hispanic Parents. *Urban Education,* 19, 145-160.

So, A. Y. (1987a, April). High-Achieving Disadvantaged Students: A Study of Low SES Hispanic Language Minority Youth. *Urban Education,* 22, 19-35.

So, A. Y. (1987b, October/November). Hispanic Teachers and the Labeling of Hispanic Students. *The High School Journal, 71,* 5-8.

Sodowsky, G. R., Ming Lai, E. W., & Plake, B. S. (1991, September/October). Moderating Effects of Sociocultural Variables on Acculturation Attitudes of Hispanic and Asian American Students. *Journal of Counseling and Development,* 70, 194-204.

Softas-Nall, B. C., Baldo, T., & Williams, S. (1997, October). Counselor-Trainee Perceptions of Hispanic, Black, and White Teenage Expectant Mothers and Fathers. *Journal of Multicultural Counseling and Development,* 25, 234-243.

Solís, E., Jr. (1995, Winter). Regression and Path Analysis Models of Hispanic Community College Students' Intent to Persist. *Community College Review,* 23, 3-15.

Solorzano, D. G. (1992). *The Road to the Doctorate for California's Chicanas and Chicanos: A Study of Ford Foundation Minority Fellows.* Berkeley, CA: California Policy Center.

Special Program Opened Their Eyes. Girls Discover They Can Do Science, Too. (1998, January). *Migrant Education News,* 9.

Stanton-Salazar, R. D., & Dornbusch, S. M. (1995). Social Capital and the Reproduction of Inequality: Information Networks Among Mexican-Origin High School Students. *Sociology of Education,* 68, 116-135.

Stavans, I. (1995). *The Hispanic Condition: Reflections on Culture and Identity in America.* New York: Harper Collins.

Steele, C. (1997) A Threat in the Air: How Stereotypes Shape Intellectual Identity and Performance. *American Psychologist* 52 (6), 613-29.

Stevenson, H. W., Chen, C., & Uttal, D. H. (1990). Beliefs and Achievements: A Study of Black, White and Hispanic Children. *Child Development,* 61, 508-523.

Steward, R. J., Germain, S., & Jackson, J. D. (1992, March). Alienation and Interactional Style: A Study of Successful Anglo, Asian, and Hispanic University Students. *Journal of College Student Development,* 33, 149-156.

Steward, R. J., O'Leary, K., & Boatwright, K. J. (1996). Social Support Networks of Successful University Students: A Study of Race, Ethnicity, and Sex. *Sociology of Education,* 68, 116-135.

Stockwell, J. (2000, April 12). The Young Voice of the Family: When Adults Can Speak Little English, Children Take on Grown-Up Role. *The Washington Post,* B.3.

Strage, A. A. (1999). Social and Academic Integration and College Success: Similarities and Differences as a Function of Ethnicity and Family Educational Background. *College Student Journal, 33* (2), 198-205.

Thorne, Y. M. (1995, September). Achievement Motivation in High Achieving Latina Women. *Roeper Review,* 18, 44-49.

Tienda, M., Donato, K., & Cordero-Guzman, H. (1992). Schooling, Color and the Labor Force Activity of Women. *Social Forces,* 71 (2), 365-395.

Tinto, V. (1997). Classrooms as Communities: Exploring the Educational Character of Student Persistence. *Journal of Higher Education,* 68 (6), 599-623.

Tomás Rivera Policy Institute. (1999, November 2). *Political and Social Issues: AP Courses in California.* Available at www.trpi.org/ap.html.

Tomás Rivera Policy Institute. *Demographic Facts and Trends.* Available at www.trpi.org.

Turner, C.S.V., & Myers, S.L., Jr. (2000). *Faculty of Color in Academe: Bittersweet Success.* Needham Heights, MA: Allyn & Bacon.

Urciuoli, B. (1996). *Exposing Prejudice: Puerto Rican Experiences of Language, Race, and Class.* Boulder, CO: Westview Press.

U.S. Census Bureau. (1993a). *1990 Census. Social and Economic Characteristics.* Washington, DC: GPO.

U.S. Census Bureau. (1993b). *We the American ... Hispanics.* Washington, DC.

U.S. Census Bureau. (1998). *Educational Attainment in the United States.* Washington, DC.

U.S. Census Bureau, Economic and Statistics Administration. (1998a). *Hispanic Population Shows Gains in Educational Attainment, Census Bureau Reports.* Available at www.census.gov/Press-Release/cb98-107.html.

U.S. Census Bureau, Current Population Reports. (2000). *The Hispanic Population in the United States: Population Characteristics, March 1999.* Washington, DC.

U.S. Department of Education. (2000). Number of Full-Time Faculty Members by Sex, Rank, and Racial and Ethnic Group, Fall 1995. Cited in *Chronicle of Higher Education Almanac, 1999-2000.* Washington, DC: Chronicle of Higher Education.

U.S. Department of Education, National Assessment of Educational Progress. (1998). Long-Term Trends in Student Mathematics Performance. In *NAEP Facts.* Washington, DC: NAEP.

U.S. Department of Education, National Center for Education Statistics. (1995). *Findings from The Condition of Education, 1995: The Educational Progress of Hispanic Students.* Washington, DC.

U.S. Department of Education, National Center for Education Statistics. (1996a). *Digest of Educational Statistics 1996.* Washington, DC.

U.S. Department of Education, National Center for Education Statistics. (1996b). *Fall Enrollment in Postsecondary Institutions, 1996.* Washington, DC.

U.S. Department of Education, National Center for Education Statistics. (1997). *Findings from The Condition of Education 1997: The Social Context of Education.* Washington, DC.

U.S. Department of Education, National Center for Education Statistics. (1998a). *Degrees and Other Awards Conferred by Degree-Granting Institutions: 1995-96.* Washington, DC.

U.S. Department of Education, National Center for Education Statistics. (1998b). *Statistical Analysis Report: Generational Status and Educational Outcomes Among Asian and Hispanic 1998 Eighth Graders.* Washington, DC.

U.S. Department of Education, National Center for Education Statistics. (1999). *Fall Enrollment in Postsecondary Institutions, 1996.* Washington, DC.

U.S. Department of Labor, Women's Bureau. (1997). *Women of Hispanic Origin in the Labor Force.* Washington, DC.

Vail, K. (1998, February). Keeping Fernando in School. *The American School Board Journal,* 185, 30-33.

Valdés, G. (1997). Dual-Language Immersion Programs: A Cautionary Note Concerning the Education of Language-Minority Students. *Harvard Educational Review,* 67 (3) 391-429.

Valenzuela, A. (1993). Liberal Gender Role Attitudes and Academic Achievement Among Mexican-Origin Adolescents in Two Houston Inner-City Catholic Schools. *Hispanic Journal of Behavioral Sciences,* 15 (3), 310-323.

Valenzuela, A. (1999). Subtractive Schooling: U.S.-Mexican Youth and the Politics of Caring. Albany, NY: State University of New York Press.

Valverde, S. A. (1987). A Comparative Study of Hispanic High School Dropouts and Graduates: Why Do Some Leave School Early and Some Finish? *Education and Urban Society,* 19, 320-329.

Vanderslice, R. (1998). Hispanic Children and Giftedness: Why the Difficulty in Identifications? *The Delta Kappa Gamma Bulletin,* 64 (3), 18-23.

Vásquez-Nuttall, E., & Romero-García, I. (1989). From Home to School: Puerto Rican Girls Learn to be Students in the United States. In C. T. García Coll & M. de Lourdes Mattei (eds.). *The Psychosocial Development of Puerto Rican Women.* New York: Praeger Publishers.

Viadero, D. (1996). Hispanic Dropouts Face Higher Hurdles, Study Says. *Education Week,* 16 (41), 3.

Walsh, C. E. (1988). "Staging Encounters": The Educational Decline of U.S. Puerto Ricans in (Post)-Colonial Perspective. *Harvard Educational Review,* 68 (2), 218-243.

Weissman, J., Bulakowski, C., & Jumisko, M. K. (1998). A Study of White, Black and Hispanic Students' Transition to a Community College. *Community College Review,* 26 (2), 19-42.

Why Hispanic-American Women Succeed in Higher Education. (1998, February 27). *Hispanic Outlook in Higher Education,* 8 (13), 12

Wiegand, D., & Ginorio, A. B. (1994). First Steps in College Science: Single Sex vs. Co-Educational Programs. Lecture at Designs for Success Conference, Mount Holyoke College, South Hadley, MA.

Winston, S. (1988, January). Office Occupations and Hispanic Girls: How to Make a Difference! *Thrust,* 17, 38-40.

Wycoff, S. E. M. (1996). Academic Performance of Mexican American Women: Sources of Support. *Journal of Multicultural Counseling and Development,* 24 (3), 146-155.

Yawn, B., Yawn, R., Brindis, C. (1997). *Adolescent Pregnancy: A Preventable Consequence?* Eugene, OR: Integrated Research Services.

Yonezawa, S. (1998). *The Relational Nature of Tracking: Using Feminist Standpoint Theory and Network Theory to Examine the Course Placement Process of 19 Secondary School Students.* Paper presented at the Annual Meeting of the American Educational Research Association, San Diego, CA. April 13-17.

Zapata, J. T. (1988, January/February). Early Identification and Recruitment of Hispanic Teacher Candidates. *Journal of Teacher Education,* 39, 19-23.

Zentella, A. C. (1997, November). Latino Youth at Home, In Their Communities, and In School: The Language Link. *Education and Urban Society,* 30, 122-130.

AAUW Equity Library

¡Sí, Se Puede!/Yes, We Can: Latinas in School
by Angela Ginorio and Michelle Huston
Comprehensive look at the status of Latina girls in the U.S. public education system. Report explores conflicts between institutional expectations and the realities of student lives, and discusses the social, cultural, and community factors that affect Hispanic education. Available in English and Spanish.
80 pages/2001.
$11.95 members/$12.95 nonmembers

A License For Bias: Sex Discrimination, Schools, and Title IX
Examines uneven efforts to implement the 1972 civil rights law that protects some 70 million students and employees from sex discrimination in schools and universities. The analysis of non-sports-related complaints filed between 1993 and 1997 pinpoints problems that hamper enforcement and includes recommendations for Congress, the Office for Civil Rights, and educational institutions.
80 pages/2000.
$11.95 members/$12.95 nonmembers. Published by the AAUW Legal Advocacy Fund.

Community Coalitions Manual With Lessons Learned From the Girls Can! Project
A comprehensive guide for establishing and sustaining effective coalition-based programs. Covers volunteer recruitment, project planning, evaluation, fundraising, and public relations, with contact information for more than 200 organizations, and lessons learned from the Girls Can! Community Coalitions Projects, a nationwide gender equity program.
168 pages/2000.
$14.95 AAUW members/$16.95 nonmembers.

Tech-Savvy: Educating Girls in the New Computer Age
Explores girls' and teachers' perspectives of today's computer culture and technology use at school, home, and the workplace. Presents recommendations for broadening access to computers for girls and others who don't fit the "male hacker/computer geek" stereotype. 100 pages/2000.
$11.95 members/$12.95 nonmembers.

Voices of a Generation: Teenage Girls on Sex, School, and Self
Compares the comments of roughly 2,100 girls nationwide on peer pressure, sexuality, the media, and school. The girls were 1997 and 1998 participants in AAUW teen forums called Sister-to-Sister Summits. The report explores differences in girls' responses by race, ethnicity, and age and offers the girls' action proposals to solve common problems. 95 pages/1999.
$13.95 members/ $14.95 nonmembers.

Gaining a Foothold: Women's Transitions Through Work and College
Examines how and why women make changes in their lives through education. The report profiles three groups—women going from high school to college, from high school to work, and from work back to formal education—using both quantitative and qualitative methods. Findings include an analysis of women's educational decisions, aspirations, and barriers. 100 pages/1999.
$11.95 members/ $12.95 nonmembers.

Higher Education in Transition: The Politics and Practices of Equity Symposium Proceedings
A compilation of papers presented at AAUW's June 1999 higher education symposium in Washington, D.C. Topics addressed include campus climate and multiculturalism, higher education faculty and success, higher education student retention and success, and the effect of equity issues on higher education curricula and classrooms.
390 pages/1999.
$19.95 members/$21.95 nonmembers.

Gender Gaps: Where Schools Still Fail Our Children
Measures schools' mixed progress toward gender equity and excellence since the 1992 publication of *How Schools Shortchange Girls*. Report compares student course enrollments, tests, grades, risks, and resiliency by race and class as well as gender. It finds some gains in girls' achievement, some areas where boys—not girls—lag, and some areas, like technology, where needs have not yet been addressed.
150 pages/1998.
$12.95 members/ $13.95 nonmembers.

Gender Gaps Executive Summary
Overview of *Gender Gaps* report with selected findings, tables, bibliography, and recommendations for educators and policy-makers. 24 pages/1998.
$6.95 members/$7.95 nonmembers.

Separated By Sex: A Critical Look at Single-Sex Education for Girls
The foremost educational scholars on single-sex education in grades K-12 compare findings on whether girls learn better apart from boys. The report, including a literature review and a summary of a forum convened by the AAUW Educational Foundation, challenges the popular idea that single-sex education is better for girls than coeducation.
99 pages/1998.
$11.95 AAUW members/$12.95 nonmembers.

Gender and Race on the Campus and in the School: Beyond Affirmative Action Symposium Proceedings
A compilation of papers presented at AAUW's June 1997 college/university symposium in Anaheim, California. Symposium topics include K-12 curricula and student achievement, positive gender and race awareness in elementary and secondary school, campus climate and multiculturalism, higher education student retention and success, and the nexus of race and gender in higher education curricula and classrooms. 428 pages/1997.
$19.95 AAUW members/$21.95 nonmembers.

Girls in the Middle: Working to Succeed in School
Engaging study of middle school girls and the strategies they use to meet the challenges of adolescence. Report links girls' success to school reforms like team teaching and cooperative learning, especially where these are used to address gender issues.
128 pages/1996.
$12.95 AAUW members /$14.95 nonmembers.

Growing Smart: What's Working for Girls in School Executive Summary and Action Guide
Illustrated summary of academic report identifying themes and approaches that promote girls' achievement and healthy development. Based on review of more than 500 studies and reports. Includes action strategies, program resource list, and firsthand accounts of some program participants.
60 pages/1995.
$10.95 AAUW members/$12.95 nonmembers.

How Schools Shortchange Girls: The AAUW Report
Marlowe paperback edition, 1995. A startling examination of how girls are disadvantaged in America's schools, grades K-12. Includes recommendations for educators and policy-makers as well as concrete strategies for change. 240 pages.
$11.95 AAUW members/$12.95 nonmembers.

Hostile Hallways: The AAUW Survey on Sexual Harassment in America's Schools
The first national study of sexual harassment in school, based on the experiences of 1,632 students in grades 8 through 11. Gender and ethnic/racial (African American, Hispanic, and white) data breakdowns included. Commissioned by the AAUW Educational Foundation and conducted by Louis Harris and Associates. 28 pages/1993.
$8.95 AAUW members/$11.95 nonmembers.

SchoolGirls: Young Women, Self-Esteem, and the Confidence Gap
Doubleday, 1994. Riveting book by journalist Peggy Orenstein in association with AAUW shows how girls in two racially and economically diverse California communities suffer the painful plunge in self-esteem documented in *Shortchanging Girls, Shortchanging America*. 384 pages/1994.
$11.95 AAUW members/$12.95 nonmembers.

Shortchanging Girls, Shortchanging America Executive Summary
Summary of the 1991 poll that assesses self-esteem, educational experiences, and career aspirations of girls and boys ages 9-15. Revised edition reviews poll's impact, offers action strategies, and highlights survey results with charts and graphs.
20 pages/1994.
$8.95 AAUW members/$11.95 nonmembers.

Order Form

Name _____ AAUW membership # (if applicable) _____
Street _____
City/State/ZIP _____
Daytime phone (_____)_____ E-mail _____

Item	Price Member/Nonmember	Quantity	Total
¡Sí, Se Puede!/Yes, We Can: Latinas in School	$11.95/$12.95	_____	_____
A License for Bias: Sex Discrimination, Schools, and Title IX	$11.95/$12.95	_____	_____
Community Coalitions Manual	$14.95/$16.95	_____	_____
Tech-Savvy: Educating Girls in the New Computer Age	$11.95/$12.95	_____	_____
Voices of a Generation	$13.95/$14.95	_____	_____
Gaining a Foothold	$11.95/$12.95	_____	_____
Higher Education in Transition	$19.95/$21.95	_____	_____
Gender Gaps: Where Schools Still Fail Our Children	$12.95/$13.95	_____	_____
Gender Gaps Executive Summary	$ 6.95/$ 7.95	_____	_____
Separated by Sex: A Critical Look at Single-Sex Education for Girls	$11.95/$12.95	_____	_____
Gender and Race on the Campus and in the School	$19.95/$21.95	_____	_____
Girls in the Middle: Working to Succeed in School	$12.95/$14.95	_____	_____
Growing Smart Executive Summary and Action Guide	$10.95/$12.95	_____	_____
How Schools Shortchange Girls	$11.95/$12.95	_____	_____
Hostile Hallways	$ 8.95/$11.95	_____	_____
SchoolGirls	$11.95/$12.95	_____	_____
Shortchanging Girls Executive Summary	$ 8.95/$11.95	_____	_____

Subtotal ($25 minimum): _____
Sales Tax: _____
Shipping/Handling (see chart below): _____
Total Order: _____

For bulk pricing on orders of 10 or more, call 800/225-9998 ext. 521.
For rush orders, call 800/225-9998 ext. 521. A $5 fee plus actual shipping charges will apply.
Shipments to foreign countries are sent surface rate and postage is charged at cost plus a $15 handling charge.
All applicable duties and taxes are paid by customer.
AAUW Federal Identification Number: 53-0025390.

❑ Check/Money Order
   (Please make payable in U.S. currency to Newton Manufacturing Co. Do not send cash.)
❑ MasterCard/VISA
   Card # __ __ __ __ - __ __ __ __ - __ __ __ __ - __ __ __ __   Expiration _____
   Name on card _____
   Cardholder signature _____

Shipping and Handling (based on order size)	
$25-$49.99	$7.95
$50-$99.99	$8.95
$100-$249.99	$10.95
$250-$350	$15.95
Over $350	$4.95 plus 5% of subtotal

SATISFACTION GUARANTEED: If you are not completely satisfied with your purchase, please return it within 90 days for exchange, credit, or refund. Videos are returnable only if defective, and for replacement only.

FOR MAIL ORDERS, SEND THIS FORM TO:
AAUW Sales Office
Newton Manufacturing Co.
P.O. Box 927
Newton, IA 50208-0927

FOR TELEPHONE ORDERS, CALL:
800/225-9998 ext. 521
800/500-5118 fax

TO ORDER ONLINE:
www.aauw.org

Foundation Board of Directors 1999-2001

Sharon Schuster, President
Mary Ellen Smyth, Development Vice President
Dian Belanger, Program Vice President
Elizabeth "Beth" Norris, Secretary
Marilyn Arp, Finance Vice President
Sally Chamberlain
Gwendolyn Dungy
Julie Englund
Jo Harberson
Jo Herber
Ruth Jurenko
Judi Kneece
Carole Kubota
Susan Nenstiel
Ann Pollina
Jeanie Page Randall
Carol Stull
Ex officio: Sandy Bernard, AAUW President

AAUW Educationall Foundation Director
Karen Sloan Lebovich

AAUW Educational Foundation Project Staff
Pamela Haag, Director of Research
Amy Beckrich, Research Assistant
Amy Robb, Librarian

The AAUW Educational Foundation provides funds to advance education, research, and self-development for women and to foster equity and positive societal change.

In principle and in practice, the AAUW Educational Foundation values and supports diversity. There shall be no barriers to full participation in this organization on the basis of gender, race, creed, age, sexual orientation, national origin, disability, or class.